D1499776

ISSUES IN MANAGEMENT–LABOUR RELATIONS IN THE 1990s

The *Issues* that are being examined include the organization, process, structure and purpose of collective bargaining; the motivations of the parties to the bargaining process; the nature, structure and evolution of the wage and salary structure; and technology-related employment issues. Changes in technology and concomitant changes in industry structure dictate changes in the structure of collective bargaining. Similarly, technology causes changes in the occupational structure of the labour force and in the sectoral and industrial structure of employment, which dictate changes in organizations, and in approaches to collective bargaining.

The dominant issue relates to power-sharing amongst the parties involved in the determination of terms and conditions of employment, which includes governments. The question arises to what extent resistance to power-sharing is motivated by management self-interest, and to what extent it is motivated by genuine concerns that the efficiency of enterprises (including institutional enterprises) will be impaired.

—

Stephen G. Peitchinis is Professor of Economics at the University of Calgary, Canada, and consultant to governments and industry on matters related to technological change and labour–management relations. He has served as Chairman of conciliation proceedings in labour–management disputes.

His previous publications include *Canadian Labour Economics, Labour Management Relations in the Railway Industry, The Attitude of Unions towards Technological Changes,* and *Computer Technology and Employment.*

ISSUES IN MANAGEMENT–LABOUR RELATIONS IN THE 1990s

Stephen G. Peitchinis

St. Martin's Press   New York

ISBN 0-312-43895-8

Library of Congress Cataloging in Publication Data
Peitchinis, Stephen G.
Issues in management–labour relations in the 1990s.
Bibliography: p.
Includes index.
1. Collective bargaining.   2. Industrial relations.
I. Title.
HD6971.5.P45 1985   331   84–26219
ISBN 0-312-43895-8

To Professor Sir Henry Phelps Brown

Contents

Introduction

A former Federal Minister of Labour of Canada, singled out three developments that were to impact greatly on the industrial relations process in the 1980s. One was *the international economic situation*, which he characterised as beset by increasing energy costs, inflation, low rates of economic growth, high rates of unemployment, and protectionist restraints in international trade; the second was *the new advances in technology* and their effect on employment, work processes, and the nature of work; and the third was *the changing meaning of work*, which was manifested in conceptions of work activity that go beyond the mere earning of an income.[1]

The first development is transitional, and as such it is not likely to remain a problem in management–employee relations: periodic declines in economic activity have been a source of conflict between management and labour and will likely remain so, as long as they present a threat to security of employment, and make it difficult for enterprises to fulfil the expectations of their employees and to meet all implicit and explicit commitments that are commonly made during periods of rapid expansion.

The second and third developments have been evolving over a number of years, and although they are not new developments, they do constitute a challenge for the 1980s and 1990s: microelectronics and communications technologies, individually and in integrated systems, will revolutionise human participation in work activity the way machines and power revolutionised human participation over the past century. The factory system, which was the outcome of machine production, contributed significantly to the emergence of labour organisations and collective bargaining; the system to emerge from the application of computer and telecommunications technology to production is yet to be determined, and the impact on employee organisation and collective bargaining difficult to predict. This suggests a precautionary and protective approach to its impacts, until such time as its permanent effects become more evident.

The issue of the changing meaning of work and attitudes towards work is not new either: increasing levels of education generally, changing lifestyles, increasing social security provisions, and changing inter-personal and personal–institutional relationships, including relationships between supervisors and supervised, teachers and learners, parents and children, will inevitably impact on the meaning of work and on attitudes towards work. But then, the concept of work itself has been somewhat uncertain, which makes the evaluation of change in the meaning of work somewhat difficult.

The integration of computer and telecommunications technology will impact significantly on the structure of industry, the organisation of institutions and enterprises, the distribution of employment amongst sectors and industries, and on the occupational structure of the labour force. Such changes will impact on employee organisations and the structure of collective bargaining. Although the nature and magnitude of the impact is uncertain, it is prudent to consider the issue of the structure of collective bargaining as a factor in the state of relations between management and organisations of employees.

Changes in the distribution of employment amongst goods-producing and services-producing industries, commercial enterprises and institutions over time suggest that labour–management relations will be subjected to increasingly critical tests, which will dictate significant changes in perspectives, attitudes and philosophies from both management and labour. Labour's employer-bashing approach will not work as the ralying slogan when the employer is the public at large, and the conflicts are with employee-managers. Employer bashing was effective when the employers were owners of enterprises, and when they were cast in the role of capitalist exploiters of workers. Owner-managers have been largely replaced by employee-managers, most of whom have the same employment relationship to the enterprise as do non-management employees: they, too, are concerned about their employment security, their incomes, their promotions; they, too, are subject to reprimands for imperfect work, for late reporting at work, for absenteeism; and they, too, would like to have more days off, longer vacations and less regimentation in the work-place. The employment relationship that separates management-employees from non-management employees is the decision-making power vested in management employees; which suggests that the most critical issue between labour and management is the issue of who makes the decisions and what procedures and processes precede the making of decisions. Notwithstanding the emphasis on changes in terms and conditions of employment when contracts are re-negotiated, the real significance will be found in changes to approaches in the making of decisions.

The attitude of management must change, too. Insolence and magisterial approaches will not work. The profiles of those opposite are changing in ways that make *them* insolent and magisterial. Management employees will increasingly confront non-management employees and employee representatives of high professional and technical status who will be disdainful of the management function. In such an environment cooperation and consent must take the place of confrontation and dictation; evidence, explanation and discussion must take the place of face value statements, accusatory pronouncements, and implied negative consequences.

The changes in employment status associated with changes in the nature of employment and in the profiles of employees will dictate changes in the wage and salary structure: the decrease in the education gap between management employees and non-management employees, and the increase in supply of potential management employees, should have a downward effect on the employment incomes of management employees. On the other hand, an upward effect should be expected if the employment status of management employees diminishes so much relative to the professional groups from which managers are selected as to cause scarcity in supply of potential managers. The wage and salary structure will be under increasing pressure to reflect market realities. On the other hand, increasing public sector employment may become manifested in increasing weight to non-market valuations.

Most works on labour–management relations have been written from the standpoint of relations between organised wage-earners and their employers. Even works on relations between public sector employees and the employing agencies and institutions have approached the issues from the traditional employer–employee, union–management model. Yet, we all know that over the past four decades the labour–management scene has been increasingly dominated not by the traditional trade unions and their industrial employers – the mining companies and their mineworkers, the automobile companies and the auto workers, the railways and the railway workers – but rather by the postal workers and the government, by policemen, firemen and other groups of municipal workers and municipal governments, by nurses and other hospital workers and hospital boards, by teachers and boards of education, by public service workers of all sorts and their government employers. Surprisingly, this change has not manifested itself in any notable improvement in the general environment of management–employee relations. On the contrary, the environment has become more confrontational; which suggests that there is more to relations between management and employees than the distribution of the ends of the economy between capital and labour.

1 The Collective Bargaining Process

INTRODUCTION

Notwithstanding the long existence of collective bargaining as a process for the negotiation of terms and conditions of employment, collective bargaining remains one of the most critical issues in management–employee relations. The terms and conditions of employment of only about half of the labour force in North America are determined by collective bargaining; in many enterprises (commercial, industrial, institutional) important employment issues are excluded from the bargaining process; and most of management continue to regard the process an infringement on its right to manage, and enter into it under duress. Simply put, most of management have not accepted fully the organisations of employees and the collective bargaining process as necessary and desirable institutions: most of them continue to regard the organisations of employees as interlopers between themselves and the employees, which impede managerial efficiency, and collective bargaining an unnecessary, protracted, costly, and inefficient process for the determination of terms and conditions of employment.[1]

This failure on the part of management to accept the organisations of employees as legitimate institutions, and collective bargaining as a legitimate process, is largely responsible for the persistence of adversarial relationships. The definition of "adversarial" is *antagonistic*: which means opposition and hostility, rooted in a sense of incompatibility. It is not a question of employee organisations demanding more and more, challenging management prerogatives, and imposing increasing costs on enterprises. Similar outcomes result from the purchase of other goods and services, at prices that are most often determined through negotiations, without the creation of animosity. The

1

problem will be found in the attitude of management towards employee organisations and employee representatives. It is a patronising attitude; an attitude of superior knowledge; an attitude of authority. Even where management representatives are inferior to employee representatives in every respect, i.e. education, income, knowledge, intelligence, and even social status, the representatives of management tend towards an attitude of authority and dictation.[2] Such an impression may be a negotiating ploy, but it tends to generate responses and an environment that are not conducive to effective negotiations.

From the standpoint of organised labour, its adversary relationship to management derives from its long and bitter struggles for organisation and recognition for collective bargaining purposes, the continuing opposition to organisation and collective bargaining in some employments, and the generally negative attitude by management towards employee organisations and the collective bargaining process.

From management's standpoint, the adversary relationship derives largely from the challenges to its prerogatives to manage their enterprises – the constraints that contractual rules and regulations impose on its freedom to manage.

Rules and regulations are most often protective devices, designed to prevent actions that will effect employees negatively. The greater the expectation of such actions without consultation, the greater the likelihood that employees will demand the incorporation of rules and regulations in the collective agreement; which means that the extent of rule-making in collective bargaining reflects the degree of adversarial relationship. The less the parties trust one another the more bargaining between them turns into a process of rule-making on every detail of the working relationship![3] Employee organisations seek to protect employees against a management which allegedly is ready to take any action against employees to advance its self-interest and the self-interest of the enterprise; while management seeks to protect the enterprise against employee organisations that are allegedly bent on its destruction. The reality that neither of them is likely to have such intent is lost in the storm of emotion.

The organisation of groups in pursuit of self-interest is widespread in our society, and generally it is not regarded negatively: professional occupations organise to advance their professional interests, to set professional standards, to regulate and control entry into their professions, to regulate the practice of their professions, to set charges for the services rendered by members of the profession, to lobby with governments for favourable legislative treatment; enterprises organise, openly and covertly, to control supply, to influence demand, to set prices (OPEC, for example), to influence public opinion in support of their self-interest, and to lobby with governments for legislative and regulatory support in the pursuit of their self-interest (which often some of them equate with the public interest); we organise into political parties to propagate our political philosophies, to gain political power and thereby attain our political goals, which, too, often serve our self-interest. Why then organisations of groups of employees in pursuit of their self-interest are often regarded negatively? Is it the manifestation of a lingering notion of the master–servant relationship that existed in the past between employers and their employees? Is it a manifestation of management's effort to cast employee organisations in a role of disruptive elements in the structure of the economy and society? It cannot be the mere fact that employee organisations impose contractual obligations on management which restrict their freedom to manage their enterprises efficiently, since all commercial contracts impose varying degrees of limitations on management activity, whether they be contracts involving bank loans, the issuance of bonds, contracts with suppliers of materials that restrict access to alternative sources of supply which may be had cheaper over time, contracts with distributors, consultants, transportation companies, and many, many other.

All contracts delimit the freedoms of the contracting parties. The moment two parties affix their signatures to an agreement, each gives-up some freedom for unilateral action. Therefore, contracts should not, in themselves, be the source of negative attitudes towards employee organisations. What is then in the organisation of employees and in the "labour contract" that is not in other organisations and in other commercial contracts? It is the notion that the labour contract is not a commercial contract. Notwithstanding the fact that the labour contract sets out the terms and conditions for the sale of labour services, which in purpose and intent is no different from a contract for the sale of labour services by engineering consultants, accounting firms and management consultants, the contract involving the labour services of employees is viewed somewhat differently from the contracts involving the labour services of non-employees. Yet, all are contracted labour services; all are motivated by a pursuit of self-interest. Why is the pursuit of self-interest positively regarded in relation to entrepreneurship and commercial transactions, and accepted as an essential element in a market economy, but implicitly denied to employees?

One difference will be found in management's perception of the organisations of labour: the organisations of employees and their officers are perceived as direct challenges on management's right to manage the enterprise. Other commercial contracts impose conditions that are related specifically to the contracted issue: the labour contract is much more pervasive. It sets out rules and regulations that effect the daily operations of the enterprise, and it gives an impression, implicitly at least, that the officers of the employee organisations seek to participate in all management decisions that are likely to effect adversely the welfare of some employees.

Another important difference will be found in management's perception of the respective relationships to the enterprise of commercial contracts and labour contracts: management perceives commercial transactions (contracts) as *contributing* to the operations of the enterprise; labour contracts are perceived as providing for the *sharing* by labour in the output of the enterprise. Bank loans are conceived as necessary for expansion in production facilities, and for the purchase of capital equipment; the purchase of engineering labour services is conceived as a potential contributor to improvements in efficiency; the purchase of managerial consulting labour services is conceived as a contributor to improvements in the organisation of production; the purchase of the services of organised employees is perceived as a cost.

This perception is manifested also in the response of management to actions of employee organisations designed to advance the interests of employees, such as the withholding of services and so-called restrictive labour practices. Generally management appear to believe that employees should not have the right to withdraw their services: governments are called upon to prohibit the withdrawal of services, and some governments have prohibited the withdrawal of services by employees providing "essential" services and by public service employees. It is quite proper for cattlemen to withhold cattle from the market to cause an increase in price; it is quite proper for producers of oil to hold back production in order to sustain a high price; and it is quite proper for farmers to cultivate less land (with government incentives and penalties) and thereby create scarcity and high prices, but not proper for labour organisations to engage in activities which create scarcity and high prices for the services of labour. It is in society's interest for business and business entrepreneurs to engage in activities which serve their self-interest; it is not in society's interest for workers to engage in activities that are designed to serve their own self-interest.

MANAGEMENT SELF-INTEREST

Opposition by management to the organisation of employees for collective bargaining purposes must be viewed in terms of self-interest. It is in the self-interest of the enterprise to deal with individual employees directly. The bargaining power of individual employees is generally lesser than that of the enterprise, which enables management to dictate the terms and conditions of employment. Furthermore, the self-interest of management itself is better served in the absence of employee organisation and collective determination of terms and conditions of employment: management then has the authority to hire and fire without explanation; has the power to discipline without challenge; the freedom to respond with "yes" or "no", "approved" or "not approved" without grievance and explanations; to pay what the market will bear; and to grant benevolently holidays, vacations, leaves, bonuses, and other benefits. Organisation and collective bargaining formalise the relationship between management and the employees as a group, and challenges management authority. Terms and conditions of employment for all employees are standardised, and decisions affecting employees and employment must be explained and defended. The "Yes and No", "approved" and "not approved" decisions must be justified. The less a decision can be explained and defended effectively, the greater the burden on the decision-maker. The tendency is then to avoid making decisions that involve "time wasting" procedures, and decisions which cannot be explained and defended satisfactorily. Management likes to convey the impression that but for such impediments to decision-making, efficiency would increase significantly. Only if they could do what they would like to do, without explanation, justification and defence! Such attitudes manifest simply the self-interest of management, which is not necessarily the interest of the enterprise.

There is no evidence that organisation and collective bargaining have effected efficiency negatively, allegations to the contrary notwithstanding. On the contrary, the standardisation of terms and conditions of employment for all employees, and the removal of hundreds or thousands of individual terms and conditions may have contributed to improvements in efficiency. Furthermore, the elimination of unilateral decisions from the work environment, which often could not be justified or defended, undoubtedly contributed to the improvement of the work environment, with positive effects on efficiency. Nevertheless, organisation and collective bargaining are regarded as impediments to management efficiency.[4] As a result, they are merely tolerated where established, and resisted where not.

THE HUMAN ASPECT OF EMPLOYMENT

Historically, the attitude of management towards the employment of people in non-managerial and professional categories has been that the enterprise was interested in the services that people could provide, not in the people as human beings. Had consideration been given to the human aspects of employment, greater account would have been taken of the working conditions under which people laboured, which often were hardly compatible with human welfare, and consultation with workers on matters of work and working would have been a natural part of the employment relationship.

Collective bargaining, and the formalisation of enterprise–employee relationships in contracts of employment, has not changed substantially the attitude of management. Employment is still conceived in terms of the purchase of labour services: when demand for services increases, more people are taken into employment; when demand decreases, the people providing the services are disemployed. The only departure from this approach will be found in relation to employees in whom the enterprise invested capital, in the form of education, training and process-specific experience. But, even in such cases, the motivation is not so much the human aspects of employment, it is rather the return to the investment, which casts employees in the role of semi-fixed forms of capital equipment.[5]

Some changes have been introduced over time which manifest the human aspects of labour services, such as improvements in working conditions, reductions in hours of work, statutory holidays and vacations, but all of these have been largely the result of actual or anticipated legislative measures and collective bargaining. There is no evidence of any fundamental change in the attitude of management that would suggest management initiatives in the direction of humanisation of the workplace.

THE PROCESS OF ORGANISATION

Throughout history management has been generally successful in its efforts to create the impression that employee organisations and collective actions were a threat to private enterprise and social order. Had they admitted that the threat was largely limited to their authority to take unilateral action on matters related to terms and conditions of employment, it is problematical that they would have elicited public support to their policy of resistance. The fiction of threat to private enterprise, and potential threat to social order from collective action, provided for many years the necessary support or neutrality of both the public and the legislative process.

The extent to which resistance to employee organisation and collective bargaining is motivated by the challenge they present to management prerogatives is evidenced in the evolution of organisation and bargaining, and in the continuing resistance by management to the negotiation of many issues that bear significantly on the welfare of employees. At the early phases of worker organisation, when legislation did not protect organisational activity, and did not compel enterprises to recognise the organisations of their employees, management simply prohibited organisational activity on the premises of the enterprise, dismissed employees who engaged in such activities, refused to recognise their organisations, and insisted on discussions with individual employees directly.[6] When organisations became firmly established, and could not be dismissed as incidental outcomes of agitation and intimidation, employee representatives were recognised as spokesmen on behalf of employees, but on the understanding that (1) employee representatives were employees of the enterprise, not "outsiders", (2) employee representatives spoke on behalf of those employees only who were members of the organisation, not on behalf of all employees, (3) management retained the right to consult any employees directly, and (4) explicit recognition of management's right to manage, which meant that there were many issues that would not be negotiable.

In their efforts to achieve recognition labour leaders were fully aware that without public support and legislative measures achievement of their goals would involve long struggles, disruptions in production activity, and considerable costs to both enterprises and employees. Hence, they focused as much attention to political activities and the political process, as on employers and management. And it is to the political process that must be attributed the existing structure in organisation and bargaining. Had it not been for the legislative requirements on organisation, recognition, representation and bargaining, labour leaders would have continued today to allocate most of their time, effort and resources to organisational activities and activities designed to secure employer recognition.

The existing system is not what it should be, as manifested by the relatively large proportion of employees who are not organised. It is not that some of the unorganised will not benefit from organisation or that they do not wish to be organised. It is rather that in the face of opposition to organisation for collective bargaining by management, organisation of employees requires dedication, effort, commitment, sacrifices and resources which do not seem as readily available today as they were in decades past.

ORGANISATION VERSUS COLLECTIVE BARGAINING

Organisation of employees for collective bargaining continues to be an issue of controversy and a source of continuing conflict. Nevertheless, it pales into insignificance when compared to the process of negotiation. To recognise or not to recognise; what, whom or how much to recognise are specific acts, given to measurement and assessment. They can be specified in statute and regulated. Negotiation is a different matter. Since the purpose of negotiation is to reach agreement on the issues subject to negotiation, it implies a process of give-and-take, which narrows the range of difference ultimately to zero. The mere act of the parties meeting together, and facing each other, is not negotiation. Equally, it is not negotiation for the parties to exchange information on their respective positions on the issues in dispute. Yet, those were the forms of negotiation in the early stages of "collective bargaining", and continue to be the forms of negotiation in enterprises where the parties have not developed mutual respect and tolerance for one another.

It is important to note that effective collective bargaining is not conditional on mutuality of interest between the parties. Indeed if their interests were the same, and they recognised them as such, there would be no bargaining, except perhaps on the methods, approaches and avenues to their attainment. Effective collective bargaining is conditional on (a) recognition by the parties that each is motivated by self-interest – the "self" broadly interpreted to constitute the institutional and other interests each party represents; (b) accord of legitimacy by each party of the other's position, regardless how unrealistic it may seem; (c) willingness to enter into discussion with an "open mind", regardless how wide the differences in the indicated respective positions; and (d) readiness to proceed in negotiations with full awareness and acceptance of the need for compromise and trade-offs.

The approach by each party to the process, and the attitude of each party towards the other, are critical to the bargaining process: a negative approach, characterised by negative expectations from the process, will yield negative results. In other words, if either or both parties approach the bargaining process as an obligatory stage in their relations, from which they expect no agreement, it is most likely that no agreement will be reached; and if management implicitly questions the legitimacy of the representatives of the employees, who in turn question the legitimacy of the enterprise or its management (private vs. public ownership, nature of representation on boards of directors, opposition to political party in power), the process will yield negative results. Existing legislation may specify that the parties must bargain "in good faith." But, can one compel good faith? What is bargaining in good faith?

The former president of the University of California, Clark

Kerr, a mediator of considerable repute, related the following true encounter:[7]

> I used to be Impartial Chairman of the Pacific Coast waterfront back when there was really class warfare. One day I had on the docket a wage reopening case that was different from the usual grievance case – or 'the beefs', as they call them. So, in my innocence, I asked the parties whether they had tried to settle the matter themselves. Had they negotiated before asking for arbitration?
>
> They looked at me in some surprise and said: 'Negotiate?' I explained that I might be somewhat old-fashioned but it seemed to me that negotiation should precede arbitration. I told them I had never yet arbitrated an issue of this sort unless the parties had first tried to settle it themselves, and I wasn't going to arbitrate this one.
>
> 'All right', they said, somewhat reluctantly, 'we'll negotiate'. I got up to leave the room to let them negotiate, but they said, 'Sit down, this won't take long'.
>
> I sat down. The representative of the waterfront employers' association leaned across the table to Harry Bridges and said, 'Mr. Bridges, we don't know what you are going to demand but, by God, the answer is no!'
>
> Then Harry Bridges leaned across the table and said, 'To tell you the truth, we haven't made up our minds on what we're going to demand but, by God, we won't take no for an answer!'
>
> Then they both turned to me and said:
> 'Mr. Impartial Chairman, here is your case. We have negotiated'.

It is commonly assumed that the parties to the collective bargaining process approach the process rationally, each having calculated the advantages and disadvantages, costs and benefits of the various actions and tradeoffs. This is the only way in which the process and its outcomes can be analysed, understood, and anticipated. To the extent that indeterminate variables enter the process and influence the outcome, such as individuals seeking personal advantage, or intervention of the political process, or resistance to interventions by the political process, rationality gives away to "irrational" actions and costly accommodation. The history of industrial conflict is replete with stoppages that can be traced to irrational motivations.[8]

MANAGERIAL PREROGATIVES

In quest of recognition and negotiation employees have been struggling against tradition and the self-interest of management, which are conceptualised in the slogan "management's right to manage". The question arises whether management can manage effectively without powers for unilateral decision-making on matters that effect the employment of employees.

Notwithstanding the long history of collective bargaining as a process in the determination of terms of employment and conditions of work, a very large number of terms and conditions that are critical to the average employee's welfare remain a *managerial prerogative* – they are excluded from bilateral determination; are determined by management unilaterally.

Although the range and scope of management prerogatives varies from industry to industry and from place to place, the following issues are commonly excluded from collective bargaining and are determined by management: the products to be produced, including their design, quality and quantity; the technology to be used – machines, instruments and their organisation into production processes; the manpower complement to be employed – numbers of employees, levels of education, training and experience, skill mix, and all other matters that relate to the characteristics of employees;[9] the organisation of work processes; the assignment of work responsibilities; investment decisions; the markets to be developed; new products to be introduced; suppliers of materials and services; and, of course, the prices to be charged for the different products. Many of these effect employment, the conditions of work, how work is performed, and the intensity of work performance and as such are of concern to employees and their organisations. Yet, management has generally taken the position that its responsibility to manage the enterprise efficiently will be impaired if it did not have the power to make decisions on such matters. *The motto is management decides and acts, the union reacts and grieves.*

Unions have grieved and even struck on many of those matters, but primarily in response to adverse effects on employment and conditions of work, not in quest of their collective determination. Even on a critical matter such as the introduction of new technology, the grieving has been in relation to its effects, and the demands have been generally limited to the negotiation of satisfactory accommodations for adversely effected employees, not in relation to its introduction.

Two fundamental questions relate to the issue of management prerogatives: one is, how much unilateral decision-making power does management need for the efficient management of enterprises; and the other is, to what extent will managerial effectiveness in the management function be impaired if discussions with employee representatives were to precede decisions on matters that effect the employment of employees. The history of management practice provides evidence of significant changes in methods and scope of management over time, involving considerable sharing of powers, without impairing the efficiency of enterprises. For example, the change from the omnipotent boss, who made all decisions, on all matters without consultation, to the management team, where power is shared, is generally regarded positively in relation to efficiency; and there is no evidence of impairment in efficiency as a direct result of the change from unilateral decision-making by management on all matters related to terms and conditions of employment, to the system of collective determination of some of the terms and conditions of employment.

In the absence of evidence that the efficiency of enterprises is impaired by consultations and collective decision-making, the insistence that the omnipotent authority of management must be safeguarded is based on considerations of managerial power, not on the consideration of the interests of the enterprise.

Collective bargaining does constitute a challenge to management prerogatives: to the extent that management makes decisions unilaterally on matters that relate to terms and conditions of employment of employees, and the introduction of collective bargaining dictates that such matters become subject to consultation, negotiation and agreement, management is compelled to give-up the making of decisions unilaterally on matters subject to negotiation.[10] In this context, management complaints about increasing erosion of managerial responsibilities simply mean that management continues to exercise unilateral authority on some matters that relate to terms and conditions of employment, but that the collective bargaining process is encroaching on them. There remain a number of matters critical to the economic welfare of employees, adjustments to changes in technology being one of the most important, which remain largely in the managerial domain. It should not be surprising that concerned employees would wish to be informed pending changes in production processes which are likely to effect them, that they should wish to be advised on the nature of adjustments that would be required of them, and that they should wish to have some sort of standing arrangement in the handling of such matters.

In the consideration of managerial prerogatives versus negotiation, the focus should be on the long run performance of the enterprise, not on the loss of managerial prerogatives. Resistance by management to the giving-up of unilateral decision-making on matters that relate to terms and conditions of employment is based on the premise that the enterprise is better served by such a system of decision-making than by a system which provides for consultation and collective determination. This has yet to be proven as a general principle. Statements to the contrary notwithstanding, there is no evidence that the transfer of decision-making from management to the collective bargaining process on matters that relate to terms and conditions of employment has impaired the efficiency of enterprises.

THE ROLE OF GOVERNMENT IN COLLECTIVE BARGAINING

The nature of labour organisation and collective bargaining at any period through history can be discerned from the nature of labour legislation then in effect. The evolution of labour organisation and collective bargaining can be readily deduced from the evolution of legislative conditions and requirements.

An examination of labour legislation over time would indicate that the organisation of employees for the purpose of collective bargaining, and the establishment of collective bargaining between employee organisations and the management of enterprises were conditional upon the resolution of a number of problems, amongst which the following were critical: (1) *freedom of employees to organise* for bargaining purposes, without direct or indirect interference from employers, governments, public institutions, legal and law enforcement authorities; (2) *protection of the organisation* from prosecution for actions of its members; (3) *determination of the legitimacy of an organisation* as representative of the employees; (4) *recognition by employers* of certified employee organisations; (5) *establishment of bargaining processes and engaging in bargaining activity*; (6) *the issues* to be bargained; (7) *the legal status* of collective agreements; (8) *the employment status* of employees who withdraw their services temporarily (strike) when agreement cannot be reached on terms and conditions of employment; (9) *the right of employees to demonstrate* the absence of employment agreement and the withdrawal of their services by picketing the employer's premises.

Effective collective bargaining is conditional on legislative attention to all of these problems: employees cannot organise under threats of dismissal; employee organisations cannot remain viable under threats of legal proceedings for actions taken by their members; negotiations cannot take place if the employer refuses to negotiate; collective agreements that are not enforceable and collective agreements that can be repudiated by either party are likely to cause more conflict than the absence of collective agreements; and employee organisations cannot survive, and collective bargaining cannot be effective if employees who withdraw their services (strike) in the absence of agreement on terms and conditions of employment were to be deemed to have quit their jobs permanently.

The acceptance by society of collective bargaining as an appropriate process for the determination of terms and conditions of employment, and the codification of the process by legislative assemblies, is based on the premise that the process will protect workers against exploitation and socially unacceptable conditions of employment, and protect society against chaotic interruptions in economic and social activity. In this context, the legitimacy of the process rests as much with employer–employee arrangements, as with the welfare of society at large. Should the employer-employee arrangements effect society negatively, society should, and must, impose such regulations as may be necessary for its protection. Lloyd Ulman put the issue this way: "To secure protection and support by the general community, any quasi-public institution like collective bargaining must not only possess an economically and politically strategic constituency, it must also be regarded as more of a social asset than a nuisance."[11] In other words, the continuing existence of collective bargaining, without interference from governmental authority, depends on the outcomes of the process: when the outcomes are negative to society at large, governments have a responsibility to intervene.

The interests of the parties to a bargaining process are not necessarily identical to the interests of society: the parties may well enter into arrangements which have negative effects on society at large. Such is the case, for example, when the parties fail to restrain in cost–price arrangements when governments and the public at large believe restraint to be necessary for general social welfare. Governments are then duty bound to intervene to protect the interests of society. Those who criticise the periodic government interventions appear to forget that there are three parties to the bargaining process, not two: society is as much a party, and has as much of a stake in the outcomes as are the enterprises and their employees. Long before collective bargaining became recognised as a socially desirable process for the determination of terms and conditions of employment, Mackenzie King wrote: "It cannot be contended that what is a matter of grave concern to the public is a matter of exclusive concern to the parties. There is no right superior to that of the community as a whole."[12] It must be admitted that such generalisation leaves the door wide open for government intervention whenever it interprets the outcomes of the process to be contrary to the public interest; it brings attention, nevertheless, to the fact that society is always a party to the bargain.

Collective bargaining is a *socially sanctioned* process for the determination of terms and conditions of employment. It is implicitly understood that the process will be free of social intervention as long as its ways, goals and outcomes are compatible with the fundamental *principles that induced society to sanction it.*

Collective bargaining cannot be free of social intervention. The outcome of the process effects prices, employment, the location and structure of industry, the distribution of incomes, taxes, economic policy, social policy, and generally the welfare of society at large. Society cannot remain indifferent to the outcomes of private processes which effect its general welfare; and most certainly it cannot remain indifferent to the outcomes of private processes which it has itself sanctioned as desirable from the standpoint of general social welfare.

In a democratic system of government, the public will not guarantee the freedom of institutions and processes which are bent on its exploitation. Therefore, the parties to a collective bargaining process must demonstrate concern for public welfare in their dealings with one another, and refrain from intentionally inconveniencing the public to gain their objectives. Such behaviour will in time bring about restrictions on their freedom.

An important characteristic of most labour and business organisations is their failure to become integrated into the institutional structure of society or to establish close links with other social institutions. Although they themselves have become institutionalised in organisation and bureaucratised in management (administration) they have remained detached from other social institutions. As a result, they are alien to most of the concerns that dominate current society, such as, adequate housing, the problems of juveniles, crime, quality of life, the environment, recreational facilities for the young, the old and everyone, and other. It is paradoxical that large organisations should not participate actively in programmes that would alleviate some of those problems. Instead, labour organisations have remained largely organisations concerned with terms and conditions of employment for their members; and business organisations have remained largely concerned with the financial viability and growth of their enterprises. Such policies may have been appropriate in the past, when society did not demand social accountability from its component parts. But this is no longer the case: increasingly society regards industrial, commercial and institutional organisations, public and private alike, as units of the social structure, which through their operations and activities contribute to society's well-being and impose costs on society. The continuing efforts of labour and business organisations to pursue their individual goals independent of society's goals, and frequently in different directions from society's goals, will lead to confrontation. The parties will not be allowed to engage in dealings with one another without government intervention, if their dealings impose unnecessary costs on society at large.

Collective bargaining is now a well established mechanism for the determination of wages and other terms and conditions of employment. But, the public-at-large has become suspicious of the process and is increasingly questioning its desirability: there prevails a view that society is the victim, and that the process of collective bargaining has been devised to accommodate the interests of labour and management at the public's expense.

Labour gets what it can; management raises prices to offset what labour got and some more; and the public bears the cost-burden. The suspicion is even greater in relation to collective bargaining in the public sector. Since governments are largely motivated by political considerations, it is feared that they will give-in to pressures and confrontations too easily, and raise taxes to offset the increase in costs.

2 Power Sharing: Protection of Self-Interest

INTRODUCTION

Let us begin with two realities: the first is that most of us are employees. Whether we are company presidents or union leaders, managers or assembly line workers, teachers or ministers of education, our wages and salaries, pensions, vacation, and other terms and conditions of employment are determined by others. We are all employees. What distinguishes us from one another in the employment situation is the degree of authority that we have over one another. Therefore, it is the exercise of authority by employees over other employees that is involved in the examination of labour–management relations. When management employees oppose the organisation of other employees in the enterprise, or reject demands for negotiation on some issue, or deny workers participation in decision-making on issues that effect their welfare, they simply manifest their unwillingness to share their authority.[1] This is as true of the manager of the profit-seeking private sector enterprise as it is of the manager of the public institution or the senior bureaucrat of a government department. Indeed, an examination of the record may establish that resistance to the sharing of authority is perhaps greater in the public sector than in the private sector. In which case we may witness more conflict in public sector enterprises and institutions than in the private sector. This is the second reality: the organisation of employees for the purpose of collective bargaining constitutes in effect a collective decision to challenge the authority of management employees who make decisions on matters that relate to the terms and conditions of employment. Resistance by the management class of employees to share authority with other classes of employees is commonly justified on efficiency considerations: every possible change in the method of decision-making which provides for consultation with non-management classes of employees is viewed a potential contributor to inefficiency. In reality, the motivating factor is the perpetuation of an organisational environment which accommodates the orientations and values of the management class.[2]

Organisations are constituted of different groups of employees, each with common characteristics, common interests, common responsibilities, and feeling common pressures from other groups. Given an opportunity, such groups would organise and collectively seek to enhance their common interests. Resistance by the management class of employees may delay the organisation of other employees within organisations, but cannot prevent it; and concentration of management authority founded on tradition, will give away to a form of dispersed authority founded on efficiency considerations. The fictional division of employees into "blue collar" and "white collar", and the attribution to each of different values, different goals, different relationships within the organisation and different expectations, has passed into history. Most of the "white collar" have come to realise that their interests do not really differ from those of blue collar workers, and that even though in working relationships many of them may be closer to the sources of managerial authority, they are subjected to the same, and in the absence of their organisation perhaps even greater, authoritarian work environment. The white collar employee who seeks advancement up the management structure will tolerate an authoritarian environment, and submit to it, in the expectation that with upward mobility the negative impacts of it will gradually diminish. But, the white collar employee who does not have such an opportunity will seek out ways to resist it; and the most effective form of resistance is through organisation.

PARTICIPATION – SHARING OF AUTHORITY

Managers who are assigned responsibility for management of human resources, conceive their task as one of the allocation of the available human resources amongst work activities on the basis of demonstrated or potential ability. In quest of this general objective they undertake to (a) determine the potential capacities of the human resources available in the organisation;

(b) develop the necessary programmes, processes and environment in which potential capacities will manifest themselves; (c) provide the programmes which will develop the manifested capacities in line with the needs of the organisation; and (d) provide and maintain a work environment in which employees can apply their knowledge efficiently and effectively. There is nothing more stifling to initiative and despiriting in work effort than employing people in work activities which do not utilise their capacities.

There would be no disagreement between management and employees on these objectives. Disagreements arise in relation to the methods used in selecting employees, the assessment of capacities, the allocation of employees to work activities, and such other decisions taken at all levels of an organisation, effecting employees at all levels of the employment structure, from the shop floor to the president's office. The question then is how are such decisions to be made, and who should make such decisions. It is recognised that in every organisation there has to be someone with authority to make a final decision. Hence, the issue perhaps is not who makes the decision, but rather the ways in which decisions are made – the discussions that lead to the formulation of decisions, and who participates in them.[3] If efficiency and effectiveness in the allocation and utilisation of human resources is the agreed upon general objective, what rational arguments would preclude the establishment of joint management–employee committees to discuss the alternative methods that are available for the attainment of the indicated objectives?

CO-DETERMINATION – INDUSTRIAL DEMOCRACY

The quest by workers and their organisations for discussions with management on all matters that relate directly and indirectly to the employment of workers has been variously categorised, depending on the scope of the demands – *industrial democracy, codetermination, worker participation, worker control.*

Industrial democracy is a broad political concept that is difficult to formulate into a functional system. According to Nobel Laureate Herbert Simon the concept derives from efforts to limit and control the authority of people over people. He writes:

The term democracy refers to the methods we have devised for controlling authority in our society as a whole. We coin the term 'industrial democracy' to designate the mechanisms to be used for controlling authority in the work place. . . . The call for industrial democracy rests, implicitly or explicitly, on the assumption that the controls over administrative authority in organisations maintained by markets and by governmental regulation are insufficient, and that, in particular, additional controls are needed to safeguard the basic human freedoms of employees. The idea of industrial democracy is that employees (in analogy with others in the state) should be able to participate directly in the decision-making process in the organisation, as a way of safeguarding their interests.[4]

Worker control has been in effect primarily in certain parts of the Yugoslavian economy. Whereas *codetermination* and *worker participation* will be found, in varying forms, in almost every establishment, in most advanced industrial countries. In some, such as West Germany, Norway and Sweden, it has been given legal status, and it is formalised into committee structures with official representation from organised labour.[5] Joint labour–management committees are concerned with matters related to plant closings, technological changes, layoffs, health and safety, physical layout of new plants, the organisation of work, and such other. In West Germany, representatives of organised labour will be found in high level decision-making bodies of most large enterprises, all the way up to the Boards of Directors. In North America, employee participation will be found largely at the shop floor, functioning on contract or ad hoc basis. What is *codetermination* on the shop floor in Europe, it is *participation* in many enterprises in the United States.[6] The difference between the two forms of relationship *at the shop floor level* appears to be one of organisation rather than one of substance.

Much has been written about worker participation and codetermination in Sweden, yet there is no conclusive evidence that workers and their organisations have any influence on important company policies. A most revealing discussion took place on the issue between US and Swedish unionists in 1981, after a visit by the US unionists of Swedish establishments. One US unionist pondered:

> Labor–management relations in Sweden have traditionally
> been somewhat less antagonistic than those in the United
> States, (and) various forms of codetermination . . . seem to
> have reduced that antagonism further . . . but have the unions
> achieved real influence in important areas? Or, on the other
> hand, does it seem that the unions are being co-opted by
> management?

Another unionist reached the conclusion that:

> Swedish unions have more information about certain things . . . in
> a lot of subsidiary areas that there is a lot of influence that is of
> interest to the union membership, *but on substantive issues* . . .
> [such as] the investment policy of the company . . . there
> wasn't a lot of progress being made through codetermination.
> It looked to me that the company determined and the union
> cooperated.[7]

It should not be surprising, of course, that employee organisations whose activities are limited to individual enterprises
should have limited influence on decisions that go beyond the
terms and conditions of employment, codetermination and worker
participation notwithstanding. Effective participation in decision-
making processes, and influence on the outcome of such processes,
depends on intensive study of the issues, and the formulation of
policy positions. Few employee organisations have the capacity
to engage in such intensive research activity, which places their
representatives in the rather embarrassing position of participation by presence in joint committees, but limited participation
by presentation of viable alternatives in the solution of problems.
A Swedish participant in the discussion cited above commented:

> the traditional union attitude is to sit in joint committees when
> the union has not got a program of its own . . . and negotiate
> when the union knows what it wants . . . When you sit in joint
> committees when the union doesn't have a real program, then
> you become co-opted. But if you do it the other way around,
> you will sit in joint committees only *after* the union has estab-
> lished its own program and really knows what it wants. *Then* they
> can sit in joint committees. But until then, negotiate.[8]

To some extent the issue of codetermination and worker participation is largely one of codification, contractual commitment and discretion: many codetermination arrangements are legislated and contracted; whereas most participation arrangements are "shop" tradition, and to some extent at the discretion of management. The issue is then whether unions regard participation sufficiently important to give it priority in the bargaining agenda, and attempt to formalise it, and incorporate it into their employment contracts. Whether they will do so will depend on what they will gain from it. Formalisation of representation on a Committee, agreement to expand the participation of labour in existing committees, and the creation of other committees, do not in themselves represent a significant gain, unless they promise improvements in the terms of employment and conditions of work. Effective representation on a health and safety committee, for example, would be valuable participation. Similarly, an agreement in the sharing of productivity gains would provide rationale for participation on a committee on productivity. But, in the absence of agreements that provide for the sharing by workers in the benefits emanating from participation, the incentive for participation and for the formalisation of the process of participation acquires social and political overtones. The participants gain personal satisfaction from the act of participation, and the illusion of co-determination.

Participation is a goal to which increasing reference is made by organised labour, but participation with objectives is being sought, not participation in the form of token representation. Participation is being sought in areas of activity which will benefit the workers, such as health and safety, the organisation of work processes, setting of work standards, productivity, and such other. The decade of the 1980s and 1990s will see these and other issues, such as technological change and the sharing of productivity gains, on the forefront of collective bargaining. But, whether worker representation on the relevant committees will be effective will depend on whether management recognises and accepts without reservation the legitimacy of employee organisations, and accords legitimacy to concerns of employee organisations for the employment welfare of employees. A case in point is the election in 1980 of United Automobile Workers Union president Douglas Fraser to the Board of Directors of the Chrysler Corporation. Was that election an aberration dictated by an isolated circumstance, or was it a recognition by management of a legitimate interest by workers in the decision-making process at the highest level? Was it a response to an isolated passing circumstance, or the beginning of industrial democracy in the United States? Opinion is sharply divided: some assert that economic and social conditions in the United States favour the evolution of industrial democracy;[9] whereas others have concluded that although some recent events give the appearance of a conducive environment, the institutional structure is alien to such a development.[10]

The institution of industrial democracy, co-determination, worker participation or whatever it might be called will not yield benefits to the enterprise and the workers until the parties to the bargaining process expunge from their respective attitudes the sense of inherent conflict, and approach issues with an attitude that is conducive to the discussion of problems and their resolution. For example, it is generally recognised by all that new technology is dictated by competition, and the quest for higher efficiency, lower costs and higher incomes. It is also recognised, however, that new technology has implications for employment, skills and the organisation of work activities. Logic would suggest no basis for adversarial approaches to the issue. However, a number of potential problems exist, which require solution: how is the technology to be implemented to minimise the adverse effects on workers and the community at large; what new skills will be required; which of the heretofore employed skills will not be required; what programmes and processes will be needed for the re-training of employees; what procedures will be used in selecting and transferring employees to alternative activites; how will work activities be organised in the new processes; what terms and conditions should exist for those whose services will no longer be required. Who should be responsible for the examination of these potential problems and the formulation of alternative solutions? Do employee organisations have a legitimate case in their claim for participation in the search for solutions?

Involvement of this nature is problem-solving involvement; it is not rule-making involvement of the nature that is common to collective bargaining. Problem-solving involvement is incompatible with adversarial postures. Points of view will differ, as they differ amongst management in relation to most problems. But, at the management level discussions are initiated and carried out with the objective of determining the nature and magnitude of the problems, the factors that cause them, and the alternative solutions. Ultimately, decisions are taken which favour the views of some and not those of others. The key is in the approach, not in the issue: the problem-solving approach involves the parties in discussions of alternative ways to reach agreement on outstanding issues; whereas the adversarial approach involves the parties in arguments on gains and losses, costs and benefits. In the problem-solving approach, agreement on changes in terms and conditions of employment are accepted as just, equitable, and of benefit to both sides – the way it is deemed when the salaries and other terms and conditions of employment of senior management are changed. In the adversarial approach, changes in terms and conditions of employment are regarded as gains to employees and costs to the enterprise. It is not possible to maintain cooperative and harmonious relationships when the parties approach each other with the expectation that the outcome of the process will result in gains and losses.

Worker participation systems are successful where a spirit of trust, mutual respect and cooperation exists amongst the parties involved – management at all levels, the employee organisation and the workers. They cannot exist in environments where there are conflicts of interest between employers and employees, management and employee organisations, and employees and their organisations. In such environments, participatory structures turn into wasteful debating forums, and rhetoric becomes a substitute for performance.[11]

It is generally recognised, of course, that the development of trust and mutual respect is a very slow process, requiring leadership, initiative, patience, and hard work. Conflicts of interest cannot be removed; they must be subordinated to the aspects of the relationship that are of mutual interest. Hopefully, attainment of the goals that are to the mutual interest will reduce the gap of self-interest. But, trust and mutual respect will not evolve in an organisational environment which keeps the parties apart most of the time, and brings them together from time to time only, when disputes need to be settled and contracts to be negotiated. It is predicated on an organisational structure that dictates frequent communication, consultation, and demonstration of confidence in the system. In addition the system must provide for widespread worker participation; otherwise, distrust can develop between workers and their representatives, which will be manifested in failures to support, implement or ratify agreements.

All evidence indicates increasing worker expectations of job enrichment, and participation in decision-making at the work level.[12] The intensity of their expectations should not be minimised by the leaders of their organisations or by management. It is incumbent on both to take the matter seriously and devise organisational structures that will give full expression to such expectations. Failure to do so will be manifested in the continuing problem of relatively low productivity, and imperfections in products and services, notwithstanding the continuous improvements in the technology of processes and products.

Co-determination arrangements of various sorts in effect at present in certain European countries have not sprung up suddenly; they have evolved over many decades within compatibly evolving social, political and institutional environments.[13] Advocates of so-called 'industrial democracy' in North America manifest an appalling degree of ignorance of the social and institutional foundation that is necessary for an effective system of co-determination. The objective is not to simply get employee representation in the Boardroom; the objective is to get business policies and practices which recognise and give adequate priority consideration to the interests of employees and society at large. Such recognition and priority consideration requires an attitude on the part of the major participants in economic and social activity, i.e. business, labour and government, that will not be obtained by the simple act of union representation in the Boardroom. Consider, for example, the case of Austria, to which frequent references are made for the absence of labour-management conflicts. "The idea of cooperation" writes a State Secretary in the Ministry of Finance "has its roots in the political and economic history of our country. The civil war and mass unemployment in the thirties, the disastrous and disillusioning experiences of the Nazi period, the occupation and the economic collapse after the Second World War – all these factors strengthened the desire of the different social and political groups to work together and to solve outstanding problems by making compromises."[14]

In addition to the existence of compatible social and political environments, the nature of employee organisations has contributed significantly to the success of co-determination in countries

such as Austria. Employee organisations have a corporate structure: their officials, not the employees, determine policies and
select representatives to boards, commissions and committees.
It is a question of considerable consequence whether co-
determination can in fact function effectively within a democratic
environment of the North American sort, where the membership of
organisations is accustomed to direct participation in the election of representatives and in the formulation of major policies in
open forum.[15]

EMPLOYEE ORGANISATIONS AND EMPLOYEE INTERESTS

A distinguished British professor of law, Sir Otto Kahn-Freund
identified two important characteristics in British labour relations: *direct democracy*, and *market and job control*. By direct democracy he meant that most important union decisions are made by
the membership, mainly at the workplace, and not by elected
union officers; whereas by market and job control he meant that
the aim of many unions has been not only to regulate the terms
of employment but also to regulate "access to jobs and of the
supply in the labour market".[16]

These are not peculiarly British characteristics, although it is
possible that greater importance is attached to them in Britain,
and they figure more in labour–management conflicts in Britain,
than they do in other developed industrial countries. Shop
stewards are more active on the shop floor in Britain than in
other countries, and there seems to be lesser flexibility in job
adjustments in Britain than in other countries. But, these are
differences in degree only, and not in the substance of the
characteristics: an examination of the processes and procedures
in decision-making by unions in North America will determine
that policies which effect the terms and conditions of employment of workers *directly* are commonly taken (approved) directly
by the workers; only policies of a general nature, involving some
expression of approval or disapproval of government policy, for
example, are taken by representatives of workers gathered together in
assembly. It is the direct involvement of the workers that gives
strength to their organisations. The organisations that are relatively weak are those which do not have direct links with the

workers, and do not receive signals from workers directly. It is not an infrequent occurrence for such organisations to call on workers to take some action, to protest against some government policy, and find themselves largely ignored. It is very seldom that workers would ignore the organisation to which they are linked directly. Few organisations are powerful in themselves; most derive their power from the direct participation of their membership.[17]

This suggests the existence of negative characteristics in the institutionalisation of organisations, and the concomitant establishment of administrative structures, and rigid rules and regulations. The focus becomes split then between the organisation as an institution, and the organisation as a collective of the membership. The extent of the split, and the direction in which the organisation will evolve depends on the abilities and personalities of the leaders, and the degree of direct involvement by the membership. For an organisation to remain a collective of the membership, the membership must participate in the affairs of the organisation actively and continuously. When the membership begins to transfer functions to officers of the organisation, who are employed by the organisation, the power of the membership begins to erode. This is particularly the case when the functions performed by such employees begin to encroach on the decision-making process. Employees of organisations tend to develop allegiance to the organisation; their interests, their advancement within the organisation are related to the size and structure of the organisation, the initiatives that are taken by the organisation, and the power structure within the organisation. Their allegiance is not to those whom the organisation represents, whether they be shareholders or dues-paying members.

The institutionalisation and over-organisation of employee organisations tends to separate the organisation from the membership. Direct participation by the membership becomes limited to periods of election of leaders and when proposed contract renewals are discussed and voted upon. In effect the process becomes transformed from direct democracy to representative democracy[18] with all the disadvantages inherent in decision-making through representation, contrasted to direct participation. Although organisation of some sort is desirable, and indeed necessary for administrative purposes when organisations increase in size, the administrative functions of the organisations must not be allowed to encroach upon the decision-making functions of the membership. The size of the organisation does not preclude direct participation; it is a matter of appropriate organisation for the purpose. What precludes direct participation when organisations increase in size is the conflict of interest between the organisation as an institution, and the membership as a collective. Ultimately, the choice of organisation should be based on which responds most effectively to the needs and expectations of the members. Modern communications technology promises easy access to all sorts of information on employment and conditions of employment for everyone. In the 1990s workers will be generally better informed, and can be expected to demand greater accountability from their leaders and organisations.

THE QUESTION OF JOB CONTROL

Amongst the issues that have caused most concern to most workers has been the issue of employment security. Fluctuations in economic activity, structural changes in the economy manifested in declines and the disappearance of goods, services and processes, the emergence of new goods, services and process, and changes in the technology of production processes, all have exposed many workers to periods of unemployment, and created a sense of employment insecurity. It is natural then that through organisation workers have sought some protection in their employment – job protection, and recognition of some right to employment, some form of property right, based on length of service. The first has been sought in various forms of job security, such as union shop and closed shop arrangements, whereas the second has been sought through seniority provisions.

In quest of job security workers have in effect sought, through their organisations, the exercise of control over the allocation of workers to jobs, and over the supply of labour in the market. That is the purpose of contractual provisions which require (a) that workers be or become members of the organisation as a condition of employment; (b) that an employer could not pay to employees hired off the market more or less than what is provided in the contract; (c) that employers train, retrain and relocate workers within their enterprises instead of replacing them from the market with workers who have desirable characteristics and qualifications; and (d) the establishment of journeymen-apprentice ratios which are designed to control the number of apprentices and hence the supply of certified specialists.

A job cannot be totally secure, of course, since it depends on the demand for what it produces and the technology and organisation of processes within which or in conjunction with which the job is performed. Changes in the products produced by the job, changes in the technology used in the job, and changes in the organisation of the processes within which the job is used, will effect the job. Hence, it is generally recognised by workers and their organisations that over time adjustments will have to be made to such changes, some of which may result in job losses. Indeed, some of the measures introduced in quest of job security may themselves become the source of insecurity. For example, an unduly restrictive apprenticeship programme may create undue scarcity in supply of journeymen, which will induce employers to search for alternative ways to produce the goods and services produced by the journeymen. The outcome may be new technology, new processes, new products, all of which may employ less and less specialised labour. The history of the printing trades comes to mind. Nevertheless, recognition of the inevitability of change over time, and the job insecurity that is associated with it, does not reduce the critical importance of measures designed to provide for job security. On the contrary, it increases their importance and compels the introduction of rules and regulations which will ensure that the adjustments are based on rational considerations, not on discriminatory characteristics.

It is noteworthy that in quest of job security, workers and their organisations are not conspiring against their employers, they are conspiring against other workers. In a true competitive spirit they are seeking in effect to impose barriers to entry into the occupations and employments which they dominate, and thereby attain, maintain and increase their privileges in employment.[19] The inconveniences they impose on employers, or the excessive, artificially created, prices they charge for their services, may be a lesser burden to society in the long run than the exclusion from jobs and employment of other workers. As indicated above, rather than providing job security, restrictive policies can become the cause of job insecurity in the long run.

Much critical comment has been voiced by employers about the constraints imposed on their freedom by job security arrangements; yet the security arrangements sought or imposed by employee organisations are no different *in purpose* than contractual, legal and administrative ways sought by employers to reduce or eliminate their own competition. The purpose is largely self-interest: whether that is manifested in the form of a closed shop, or the imposition of a high tariff to eliminate external competition, or a collusive arrangement between established competitors to bar an increase in competition, the purpose is the same – to protect and enhance one's self-interest. It would be unjust to single out unions as the only or the major perpetrators of restrictive practices designed to provide job security and improved earnings. Indeed, many of the professions are more notorious in this respect than the unions of wage-earners: one cannot go to a medical specialist directly, regardless how obvious that the malady requires the services of a specialist; one cannot purchase a stock directly from the stock exchange, one must go through a broker and pay a fee; the intricacies of law and courts of law dictate the employment of a lawyer, even though the case may not be contested and may involve a simple procedure; etc.

There is no doubt that many rules, regulations and customary practices can be defended on the basis of the public interest, but upon careful examination it will be determined that for the most part they are motivated by the self-interests of institutions, managers and administrators, workers, union officials, professional practitioners, bureaucrats, political functionaries and others who find security and advantage in the established order of things. Recognition of this reality by those who function within the established order of things, can be expected to reduce significantly the sense of outrage they feel, although not necessarily their opposition, towards those who seek changes in the rules and regulations which will advance their self-interest. The advance of self-interest is an important tenet of the free enterprise system. Recognition of it as the motivating factor in quests for changes in rules, regulations and methods of governance on the part of some, and resistance to changes on the part of others, will provide a more rational perspective to the discussions.

Conflicts on the issue of power-sharing are potentially more serious than conflicts over the sharing of the income pie:

increasing claims on the income pie have been met over time through increases in prices, substitution of labour with capital, reductions in employment, increases in productivity, changes in products, and scores of other ways. Claims on power cannot be offset so easily: to management, there are no offsets to the sharing of power in the decision-making process.[20] Claims to the contrary notwithstanding, it is not the distribution of the income pie, conditions of work, tradition, customs or culture that preclude the evolution of greater cooperation in relations between management employees and non-management employees. The major obstacle is the pursuit of self-interest by both sides.

3 The Structure of Collective Bargaining

Bargaining structure commonly means the size and scope of organisations engaged in collective bargaining. Arrangements vary from the highly decentralised, where the organisation of a single skill bargains with each and every employer of that skill in turn, to the highly centralised, where a federation of employers bargains with a federation of employees. The first is quite common in North America, while the second is common in Scandinavian countries. In relation to the United States, John T. Dunlop wrote: "Perhaps the most significant characteristic of the American collective-bargaining system is that it is highly decentralised."[1]

The nature of bargaining structure, whether centralised or decentralised, has important implications for the outcomes of the bargaining process. For the United States, Daniel Mills found a close relationship between the degree of centralisation in the bargaining structure and the frequency in strike activity – the more decentralised the bargaining structure, the greater the strike activity.[2] For Canada, Stuart Jamieson attributed at least some of the frequency of strike activity to "the highly decentralised trade union movement".[3] On the other hand, Weber has argued that centralisation in the bargaining structure may result in loss of influence by workers over the terms and conditions of employment that are being negotiated by their organisations, which, if allowed to develop into widespread dissatisfaction, may also result in an increase in strike activity.[4] Similarly, a Canadian Task Force on Labour Relations expressed concern that centralisation may result in "absentee decision making", dissatisfaction by the rank and file, and conflict.[5] Its report refers to a Task Force study which found "a significant correlation between the remoteness of decision making and labour-management conflict: that is, the further away from the workers a decision is taken, the greater the possibility of conflict".[6]

Even where employees are organised in one union, as in the case of public service employees, and that union is responsible for bargaining on behalf of all groups of employees that constitute it, if individual units within it are certified for bargaining purposes the union will be able to bargain for each group of employees in turn, and thereby be in a position to disrupt work activity as many times as the number of certified groups on whose behalf it negotiates.

In relation to the United States, Herbert Northrop wrote the following:

> The structure of collective bargaining in the United States is a fascinating polyglot of craft, industrial, local, regional, national and miscellaneous arrangements that derive from history, accident, ambition, relative power, government interference, and a host of other factors.[7]

In a system where a number of unions negotiate together with individual employers or groups of employers, the number of bargaining units within each establishment does not matter. The initial negotiations about terms and conditions of employment that each bargaining unit seeks for its members take place within and among the participating bargaining units and not with the employer. What is taken to the bargaining table for negotiation with the employer is a package on which all bargaining units have agreed. Whatever battles for union leadership and privilege are waged by individuals, individual units, occupations or groups of employees are waged within their organisations and during inter-organisational negotiations in the preparation of the package, and not during negotiations with the employer. By contrast, when each bargaining unit seeks a separate contract, each takes to the bargaining table its own package, and each, in turn, can disrupt operations.

The pressure for the preservation of small bargaining units emanates mainly from leaders and aspiring leaders of groups of employees who are united with some common employment characteristics, and from groups of skilled employees who seek to obtain or attempt to preserve some special recognition and privileges.

On the other hand, inter-union rivalries, and decreasing memberships in occupational and industry unions facing declining employment would tend to encourage mergers. The self-interest of union officers and professional union staff would dictate efforts at amalgamation of such unions. A study of union mergers in the United States found four positive influences: pressures from within the labour movement to reduce inter-union rivalries; efforts to increase the bargaining powers of individual bargaining units; a response to declining memberships and union revenues, because of declining employment in some skills and industries; the increase in power for some union officers, and increase in employment security, pay and positions for some professional union employees.[8] These positive influences have their negative sides, of course: mergers entail the loss of independence; often they involve the loss of identity for the craft; they compel sacrifices of craft interests for the good of the merged organisation; and the self-interest of some union officers and professional union staffs would dictate opposition. It is well known that in mergers some gain and some lose. The potential losers can be expected to react negatively to attempts by the potential gainers. The large number of unions in existence within individual industries and institutions would suggest that potential losers have been the winners, notwithstanding the considerable advantages of united organisations.

From the standpoint of bargaining power, there is no serious disadvantage in having a multitude of bargaining units within each establishment, if all of them were to bargain together on terms and conditions of employment common to all of them. Indeed, there is considerable merit in bargaining units that are constituted of employees with common employment characteristics: they are bound together by common interests; their leaders remain attuned to the problems and wishes of members; and being cohesive groups, they provide a degree of stability in the labour force. It is when each of them seeks a separate contract that problems arise.

"INDUSTRY-WIDE" AND "MULTI-UNION" BARGAINING

Whenever operations of enterprises are disrupted in succession by different employee organisations, particularly the operations of public sector enterprises, such as airports, docks, the transportation of grains or postal services, pronouncements are made about the desirability of "industry-wide bargaining" as a possible corrective system. What is being suggested is joint negotiations by all bargaining units in existence within individual enterprises, i.e. that all bargaining units within the post office, airports, docks, join together for bargaining purposes. This is multi-union bargaining, not necessarily industry-wide bargaining. "Industry-wide" bargaining could involve one employee organisation negotiating with all employers who constitute an industry, i.e plumbers negotiating with an association of building contractors. "Multi-union" bargaining would involve all employee organisations within a given enterprise, negotiating jointly with the employer of their members. There could be, of course, multi-union/industry-wide bargaining, where all or a group of employee organisations in a given industry, i.e. railway industry, mining industry, construction industry, join together to bargain with all or a group of employers of their members.

Therefore, when reference is made to industry-wide bargaining as a possible solution to the problem of successive interruptions in operations of individual enterprises such as airports, postal services and others, what is actually meant is multi-union bargaining. In other words, if one could get all employee organisations at the docks, the airports, the post office to join together for bargaining purposes, the possibility of successive interruptions in operations by different employee organisations will be reduced significantly.

CONCURRENT INDUSTRY BARGAINING

Another source of interruption in the operations of individual industries is the inter-industry operational dependence that is such a common characteristic of specialised industrial systems. Most industries are linked operationally to other industries, and depend on them for supplies of materials, parts and services. Interruption in the operations of any of them will impact on all in varying degrees, depending on the nature of operational dependency. In view of this, some sort of coordination in industry bargaining may be desirable to minimise the number of potential interruptions over time. To this end it is often suggested that such operationally linked industries begin negotiations at the same time and enter into agreements of equal duration.

The argument takes the following form: the joining together of bargaining units within an enterprise for bargaining purposes removes the potential of interruption in operations by each bargaining unit in turn; and the joining together of all enterprises that constitute an industry and all unions in the industry in industry-wide bargaining, removes the potential of frequent interruptions within the industry.

There remains then the problem of interruptions the result of inter-industry links – a problem that is critical to industries whose operations are dependent on the operations of other industries. For example, the joining together of all railway unions for bargaining purposes reduces the potential of each railway union disrupting the operations of the railway in turn; and the joining together of all railways and their unions in industry-wide bargaining reduces the potential of each railway being interrupted in turn. There remains the problem now of interruptions in industries to which the railways are linked operationally, such as docks and grain elevators, for example. The coordination of bargaining amongst such industries, particularly in relation to commencement of negotiations and duration of contracts, is one possibility. Another possibility is some sort of *sectoral bargaining* which would involve all industries and labour organisations that are dependent on one another for their operations.

Where the production and distribution of essential goods and services is carried out successively by a number of industries, and as a result interruptions in any one industry in the chain causes a standstill on the whole process, it might be desirable to have *concurrent bargaining* in the entire process. For example, the transportation of grains to foreign markets, has been interrupted by railway workers, grain inspectors, longshore foremen, longshoremen, grain handlers employed in elevators, weighmen and samplers, clerks and a score of other groups on the chain.

But, before the structure of collective bargaining can change from the relatively decentralised system in effect at present to a more centralised one, organisational structures, methods of governance and decision-making must change in such a way as to guarantee the identity and welfare of groups of employees that are united by common characteristics of skill and employment. It is the dissatisfaction of such groups with their status and influence within larger units that initiated and fostered the trend toward decentralisation;[9] which suggests that as long as specialised groups of employees remain apprehensive about their status and influence in the decision-making processes of multi-unit bargaining groups, they will not participate.

Centralisation in bargaining need not mean, of course, amalgamation of employee organisations into federations. Although this has taken place in the past, and industrial unions are a good example, what is being suggested is the formation of company-wide or industry-wide confederated employee organisations for the negotiation of master contracts. Over time, as differences in bargaining aims and objectives are resolved and common philosophies evolved, amalgamation into federated organisations may come about automatically. Furthermore, amalgamations or joint multi-union negotiations may be dictated by microelectronic links of industries and institutions, which will establish operational inter-dependencies. Members of individual bargaining units would not wish to be deprived of employment every time that some unit interrupts the process of the entire system.

LOCAL PROBLEMS, LOCAL NEGOTIATIONS

Regardless whether bargaining units federate or confederate for bargaining purposes, the resulting centralisation in relations between employee organisations and employers must not deprive local officers from participation in the negotiation and resolution of local problems.[10] Consolidated bargaining will not resolve problems that relate to employee disaffection and cannot be designed to deal successfully with strictly local issues. Local issues can only be resolved locally, by those directly affected. For example, grievances that relate to conditions of work in a given plant or office should be examined and resolved by the parties within that plant or office. No one knows better the actual impact of the physical, operational and human environment than those who work within it; and no one can appreciate more the effect of change than those effected by it. Consolidated bargaining is more likely to be acceptable and more likely to be successful if the issues for joint negotiation are limited to those which are generally recognised as being common to the employment security and economic welfare of all employees – the redundancy effects of technological change, separation pay, standard rates of pay, pensions, health, vacation, retirement and such other. Working conditions, shop and office rules and regulations, and such other issues that relate to the daily work-lives of employees should be left as much as possible to joint labour–management committees at the local level of the bargaining structure.

ORGANISATIONAL TRENDS

The current trend in the United States appears to favour consolidations in bargaining, organisational mergers, company-wide bargaining and even industry-wide bargaining; on the railways, in transport, in steel, nickel, aluminum, in the automobile, farm implement and aircraft industries, and in many other, negotiations are carried out on behalf of multitudes of occupations and employment classifications.[11] In some instances entire industries are involved, in some entire multi-plant and multi-office companies, and in some negotiations with the individual companies of an industry are carried out so closely together in time-interval, and the issues are so similar, as to constitute in fact industry-wide bargaining. Only employee organisations in certain parts of the public sector and in the construction industry appear to be resisting the trend, although pressures for consolidation are in evidence here, too. It is only a matter of time, and strong consolidation-minded leadership, before it is brought about.

The increasing complexity of the economic and social environment, the instant exposure to public view via television of actions taken by parties to disputes, the increasing need for resources and staff for research preparatory for negotiations, will bring about further centralisation and consolidations. The need for additional financial resources is becoming critical with many organisations: operational and organisational costs have risen substantially in the past few years and continue to rise, yet members have not been inclined favourably to proportionate increases in dues. Organisations that experience constant or falling membership have only one other avenue to financial solvency and that is mergers.

Another source of pressure toward organisational consolidations and centralised bargaining is the general social and political environment. Individuals who accept leadership roles, whether in business, government or institutions are now expected to consider the effect of their private institutional and organisational policies and actions on general public welfare. Wages, prices, rents, production, consumption, extraction and use of natural resources, are viewed in relation to economic growth, social costs and benefits, conservation and the physical environment; they are no longer private matters. The traditional posture of employee organisations that employers act whereas they merely react is no longer acceptable to the general public. They are viewed as social, economic and political institutions whose policies and actions affect not only the enterprises and institutions with which they bargain, but also society at large. As such they are identified with, and are expected to identify themselves with, the general economic and social results of their aims, objectives and actions.

Such social expectations of organisational behaviour are becoming a source of conflict within organisations and between organisations: it is a conflict between "the public be damned" groups and those who believe that overt demonstrations of awareness and consideration of general public welfare will bring about greater benefits in the long run. The former generally favour independent action to obtain their immediate economic objectives; whereas the latter are more inclined to seek out cooperative approaches. The prevailing social and political environment favours the latter.

SUMMARY COMMENTS ON CENTRALISED AND DECENTRALISED BARGAINING

In conclusion, it may be desirable to note some of the major advantages and disadvantages or difficulties in centralised and industry-wide bargaining:

1. Industry-wide bargaining removes from individual companies the competitive pressures that would otherwise compel or favour settlement without interruption in the production process.
2. Industry-wide bargaining removes the possibility of the employee organisation(s) concluding a favourable contract

with the weakest company or the most profitable company of the industry, and then seeking to impose the same provisions on all other companies of the industry.

3. Companies have different capacities to accommodate the demands of the employees. Therefore, when all companies of an industry negotiate together there arises the problem of differing abilities to bear the incremental burden: whatever median or average conditions are agreed upon they are likely to be higher than what the weakest amongst them can afford and lower than what the strongest amongst them can reasonably bear. In the history of industrial relations there are many instances in which employee organisations negotiated with the most able to pay and then imposed the agreements on the not so able to pay thereby causing the absorption of the latter by the more efficient. The coal mining industry of the United States is a prime example of this.

4. From the employee's standpoint, industry-wide bargaining has the advantage of industry-wide shutdown in case of failure to reach an agreement. But,

5. It has the disadvantage of inability to use one company against another either as market competitors or as examples of comparative settlements, and the further disadvantage of not being able to use dues revenue from working members to finance strike action by other members. Industry-wide shutdown does have the serious implication for many employee organisations of a virtually total stop in dues cash flow.

6. Successful joint multi-unit bargaining requires strong leadership and commitment on the part of all units to adhere to the agreed upon package. Difficulties arise when individual units seek to negotiate separately or reach "Understandings" on issues over which a common position could not be agreed upon and therefore were left out of the package.

7. Bargaining units participating in joint negotiations must be willing to give up some of their autonomy, and subordinate some of their aims and objectives to the commonly evolved aims and objectives. This is a natural consequence of any group action: every time that one elects someone else to act on his or her behalf, one loses some autonomy – some of the freedom for individual action is given up. The same applies to joint actions by groups: the formulation and pursuit of common goals requires the giving up of some individual choices.

THE DURATION OF COLLECTIVE AGREEMENTS

The length of collective agreements has been a frequent source of conflict: management has generally favoured long-term contracts, whereas labour's preferences have tended to vary over the business cycle – short-term in periods of rising prices, and when general optimism prevails in the economy, long-term when expectations are generally negative.[12]

It is not difficult to find rational explanations for the respective positions: knowledge of labour and labour related costs over relatively long periods enable management to plan operations with greater certainty. Where labour and related costs constitute a significant proportion of operating costs, uncertainty as to what they will be in two or three years is an important imperfection in the projection of costs, prices and profits. At the same time, uncertainty about economic conditions, price and wage trends dictate to labour leaders a cautious posture, particularly when the trend of wages and prices is upward and the uncertainty relates to their respective magnitudes. Good long-term contracts are not as vivid in the memories of workers as are bad ones; and many labour leaders remember well the long term contracts that appeared very good at the time when concluded, but which turned out very bad relative to the actual levels of wages, prices and profits over subsequent years.

The advantages and disadvantages that the respective parties see for themselves in short-term and long-term contracts are related, of course, to their respective expectations regarding enterprise operations and the ability to bear the indicated costs. Contracts relate to the future and their contents must reflect future operational realities, notwithstanding references to past performance during negotiations. It is departures of future realities from past expectations that have caused problems to both management and labour leaders, and it is the possibility of departures that cause them to declare their respective preferences.

THE RE-OPENING AND RE-NEGOTIATION OF AGREEMENTS

Whenever future realities have turned out significantly different from past expectations, the parties have found themselves under pressure to seek appropriate accommodation. The most recent such development was in 1982 and 1983, when a number of enterprises sought the re-opening of collective agreements and their re-negotiation in the face of unexpectedly sharp declines in economic activity. There have been instances in the past when labour leaders sought the re-opening and re-negotiation of agreements, particularly in periods of unexpectedly rapid increases in prices, and the resultant erosion in the purchasing power of agreed upon increases in pay.

When consideration is given to the possibility of re-negotiation of an employment contract, the question must necessarily arise what other commercial contracts are being or will be re-negotiated to accommodate the unexpected economic reality. The employment contract is commonly only one of a number of contracts to which parties are committed for varying periods: contracts with banks and other financial institutions which stipulate the rates of interest and payments; rental contracts; contracts with suppliers of materials; and many other. It is common to regard the labour contract more flexible than other commercial contracts, and as a result more liberties are taken in relation to it than in relation to other commercial contracts. Yet, the labour contract relates to the employment of human resources and as such should be the last to be negatively effected by unexpected negative developments in the economy.

Re-opening and re-negotiation of employment contracts is not a desirable response to economic realities that depart significantly from economic expectations. The stability inherent in a fixed contract will be destroyed, and the bargaining process will itself become unstable and uncertain. If re-negotiations were to become widespread, the outcomes of the bargaining process will come to be regarded tentative, to be re-negotiated when circumstances warranted. The development of such an attitude will create havoc with collective bargaining.

At present, provisions for the re-opening of contracts exist in relation to proposed technological changes, and some unions have succeeded in getting contracts re-opened to negotiate offsets to the erosive effects of rising prices. There have been a few instances also in which companies took the initiative and adjusted wages upward to offset the increases in prices. Nevertheless, the art of accurate predictions or projections in variables that are relevant for employment contracts is still rather primitive. As a result, negotiations are conducted in an environment of uncertainty; and uncertainty dictates the taking of risks. One cannot help but sympathise with union officers who assume the responsibility to commit hundreds or thousands of workers to fixed schedules of wages and other terms of employment for periods of two or more years. Therefore, procedures should be agreed upon for the general re-opening of contracts when conditions change so significantly as to impose serious burdens on workers and enterprises alike.

CONTINUOUS BARGAINING: MASTER CONTRACT AND SUPPLEMENTARY CONTRACTS

Contracts of short duration will involve the parties in almost continuous negotiations, which is deemed costly and bothersome. Yet, continuous negotiations will dictate the establishment of a system of continuous communication between representatives of management and of the employees, which should be viewed as an advantage to labour–management relations.

Continuous negotiations will undoubtedly bring about significant changes in the practice and form of collective bargaining: instead of negotiating on all terms and conditions of employment at the same time, and for the same period of time, consideration may be given to the grouping of issues into short-term issues and long-term issues. *The short-term* issues group could contain issues which are affected by fluctuations in economic and industrial activity; whereas *the long-term* issues group could contain issues which are not affected by short-term changes in the economy and industry, and which are not linked to the short-term issues. The former could be entered into a *Master Contract*, and negotiated as frequently as is compatible with administrative and operational efficiency and employee welfare; whereas the latter could be incorporated into a *Supplementary Contract*, and negotiated item by item or in small groups of related items at any time and for whatever period appears appropriate for the item. For example, a pension plan can be negotiated for a different duration than a health plan; and the standard hours of work could be agreed upon for a different period than the length of holidays with pay or the number of statutory holidays. Such exclusion of some items from the Master Contract and their negotiation, individually or in small groups of related items, at any time and for different periods, will result in more frequent interaction between representatives of labour and management, and facilitate perhaps a better understanding between parties, and lead to more harmonious relations.

Management and employee representatives have expressed three reservations on the issue: (1) continuous bargaining may create an environment of perpetual instability in labour-management relations and foster continuous turmoil. The all-inclusive fixed term contract, even if concluded after prolonged negotiations and a strike, has the advantage of ensuring uninterrupted operations until its expiration. Continuous negotiations will preclude such stability.

This is a legitimate concern. But given the will to cooperate in the establishment of an organisational structure for continuous interaction and negotiations, it should not be difficult to agree upon procedures which would remove the possibility of disruption in operations. For example, it could be agreed that resort to strike or lockout would be limited to disputes arising in relation to the Master Contract only. This will place the onus on labour to decide which of the many contractual issues warrant strike action as the ultimate instrument in negotiations, and which are not sufficiently important or urgent to justify resort to such action.

(2) Concern is expressed also about the possibility that continuous negotiations and removal of the strike instrument from some issues would cause problems to drag on, and result in the accumulation of unsettled issues. This potential difficulty, too, could be resolved through procedural changes: the parties could agree, for example, that failure to reach agreement on a given issue, by a given date, would make the issue subject to compulsory arbitration. Such an agreement should in no way interfere with free collective bargaining, since the decision will rest entirely with the parties themselves.

(3) Concerns have been expressed that the separation of negotiable issues into Master Contract and Supplementary Contract will reduce the range of trade-offs and thereby impede the bargaining process. Effective collective bargaining and harmonious relations depend, amongst other matters, on the joint consideration of all issues that effect the terms and conditions of employment of employees. Therefore, there should be no organisational or procedural barriers to negotiation on any issue and to trade-offs amongst issues. The grouping of issues "for Master

Contract" and "Supplementary Contract" should in no way prevent the parties from making cross references and seeking tradeoffs.

The suggested changes contain a number of potential improvements in labour–management relations: (i) negotiations on important short-term issues, such as wages would not be prolonged by haggling over issues on which agreement by a given date may not be critical; (ii) continuous communication and interaction would evolve between representatives of labour and management, thereby providing an opportunity for a better understanding of each other's problems and positions; (iii) an opportunity should be provided for the discussion of issues when they arise, thereby removing the problem of their accumulation, and the accumulation of frustrations related to them; (iv) issues and problems related to personnel administration and human resources development would be removed from their rigid legal contractual bindings and placed into a more human relations social framework; and (v) finally, the system should provide leaders of labour organisations an opportunity for continuous involvement in matters related to the employment of members of their organisation.

The last point is of critical importance to the improvement in labour–management relations: continuous involvement with matters related to the employment of those whom they represent, and continuous communication with representatives of management for the discussion of issues and problems as they arise, will make the representatives of labour more knowledgeable, will broaden their perspectives in relation to the nature and operation of their enterprises, and generally provide opportunities for the development of expertise in leadership, negotiation, and counselling. Ambitious leaders have been known to take advantage of relatively ignorant associates and use them for their own purposes; and knowledgeable associates have been known to control, replace and banish leaders whose personal ambitions conflicted with the interests of their organisations and members. Management should realise that inadequate knowledge on the part of labour's representatives, about the enterprise, the employees, the production processes, products, markets and policies, is an imperfection in the bargaining process. Communication cannot be effective when one of the parties does not have the information and knowledge on which the other party bases its argument.

THE RATIFICATION OF AGREEMENTS BY EMPLOYEES

The requirement for employee ratification of collective agreements is the only effective control employees have over their elected and appointed representatives: the quality of their selected leaders and appointed officers is tested by the contents of employment contracts they negotiate; and the ratification process gives employees an opportunity to express themselves on the issue. The ratification of proposed agreements is commonly interpreted to constitute approval of the organisation and its leadership; whereas rejection is interpreted to mean that the negotiating committees failed to communicate adequately with the membership in the course of negotiations, or failed to assess accurately the minimum expectations of the employees, or events were moving so fast, particularly in relation to the conclusion of agreements in related industries and institutions, that it was impossible to determine what terms and conditions employees would accept.

To date there has not been any authoritative examination of the reasons for the increasing frequency of employee refusals to ratify contracts recommended to them by their negotiating committees. A number of studies were carried out in the United States, and although there exists some disagreement amongst researchers, their findings are illuminating: W. E. Simkin[13] concluded that rejections were caused by (a) conclusion of agreements at some distance from where the majority of employees were working; (b) internal union politics; and (c) dissatisfaction of special groups of employees within the organisation. On the other hand, Donald R. Burke and Lester Rubin[14] examined forty-one contract rejections and found twenty-one causes mentioned in them. Amongst the most frequently mentioned factors that influenced workers in their votes were:

Ineffective communication of the terms of the proposed contract	28 times
Other union(s) from outside involved	13 times
Bargaining Committee—membership communication gap	10 times
Poor Labour–Management relations	9 times
Youth vs. Age	6 times

Local–International conflict	4 times
Other union(s) within the plant	4 times
Union elections	4 times
Misunderstanding of provisions	3 times

Evidently the most important cause appears to have been the failure of union leaders to communicate effectively the terms of proposed agreements.

Reference is made elsewhere in this book to the fact that workers are increasingly demonstrating their determination to participate more actively in the formulation of the terms and conditions of their employment. The evidence appears to suggest that they are increasingly reluctant to let the officers of their organisations determine what terms and conditions are possible. This suggests a difficult task ahead for officers of employee organisations: to provide leadership in increasingly complex economic and social environments they must set goals and objectives; at the same time they must realise that many members in their organisations are equally or even more knowledgeable about matters related to the goals and objectives than they themselves are; and therefore, they must develop effective means of communication with the membership at large, and must demonstrate readiness and willingness to communicate. Although officers of employee organisations have been known to complain that employees do not seem to recognise the existence of limits to consultation in the process of preparation for negotiations and during negotiations, there is a general basis for suspecting that perhaps less consultation takes place than conditions permit.

This relates to the demonstrated preferences of what appear to be a majority of employees; it does not relate to the preferences of extremists. There are officers of employee organisations who regard consultations of any sort as interference with their responsibilities to formulate and negotiate the best terms and conditions of employment possible within the framework of a strong and viable employee organisation; and there are employees who insist on continuous consultations in the formulation of terms and conditions of employment and during negotiations. They would not allow their negotiating committee to agree to any change in the original demands without prior approval of the membership. Such a requirement may relieve negotiating committees of the onerous task of having to keep their fingers on the membership pulse throughout the negotiations, but it would inevitably stretch periods of negotiation. On the other hand, if issues were to be divided in Master Contract and Supplementary Contract groups as recommended above, there may not result any substantial prolongation in the negotiating period.

Nevertheless, increasing numbers of officers of employee organisations are reaching the conclusion that more consultation with the membership must take place during negotiations with management, if membership rejections of contract proposals are to be reduced. Although some of them have interpreted this to mean "power to demand but not to negotiate", the extent to which they can actually negotiate will depend upon their demonstrated abilities to negotiate acceptable terms and conditions of employment, and the extent to which they have earned the confidence of the majority of members.

The president and business agent of a union local confided recently that the most difficult and depressing part of his job as union officer was the suspicion by increasing numbers of workers, particularly amongst the young, that "I might sell them cheap to management." "Regardless how good a contract or work arrangement I might succeed in negotiating", he said, "they will complain and accuse me of not having the guts to stand up to management. It is this constant suspicion, this lack of trust that gets me". Yet, when asked to what extent he consulted with the membership in the course of negotiations, he responded that there was no time and did not think it appropriate that he should consult in the course of negotiations. "It is my job" he said, "to negotiate a satisfactory contract. If they don't like it, they can reject it at ratification time."

At least this officer believed in membership ratification of agreements. He thought it essential for the maintenance of democratic processes and procedures within employee organisations. Furthermore, the requirement ensures that officers will not subordinate the employees' interests to the interests of the organisation. This is particularly important in situations where negotiating committees are constituted largely or substantially of officers from national or regional offices of organisations. Such officers are not knowledgeable of local conditions, and cannot appreciate their significance to those who work within or under those conditions. Also, in the absence of such a requirement officers can easily become remote from the membership and their problems. Participation in organisational affairs will not be obtained if participation is limited to election time only. This is, of course, what some officers desire.

Some union officers believe that the requirement for membership ratification weakens their bargaining power, enables management negotiators to approach bargaining sessions in a tentative manner, casts an air of uncertainty over the proceedings, and causes emphasis to be put on immediate gains at the expense of long term benefits. Allegedly employee negotiating committees find themselves compelled to think not only in terms of what is possible for the immediate and long term future, but also in terms of what would be acceptable to the majority of employees. This implies of course, a difference of opinion between leaders and members regarding the most desirable terms and conditions of employment. It is the task of leadership to formulate goals and objectives, explain them to members and persuade members to offer their support. Failure to gain the required support means either failure in the task of leadership or actual weaknesses in the goals and objectives.

It is also alleged that the rank-and-file cannot vote rationally on the results of proposed agreements, because they do not have the background knowledge on the nature of discussions with management representatives and on the nature of choices that had to be made. Without the knowledge of factors that shape the results of negotiating proceedings, it is not possible to determine rationally the proper place of those results in the range of possibilities. This is, of course, a standard argument of political functionaries and bureaucrats who do not wish to consult with constituents. The proper solution to a problem founded on inadequate knowledge or imperfect knowledge is to remove the inadequacy or imperfection and not to exclude from participation those whose knowledge is inadequate or imperfect.

From management's standpoint, the prevailing view appears to be that employees' negotiators should have the authority to conclude agreements. The absence of such authority casts too much uncertainty over bargaining proceedings. The game of give and take cannot be played with the degree of finality that is required in the conclusion of a contract when the party that will rule on the acceptability of the contract is not a participant in the game. On the other hand, management have been known to complain that their reasonable offers were being rejected by the executive officers of employee organisations without reference to the employees. The implication being that the employees were likely to respond more favourably.

Management's attitude on this issue appears to be governed by the nature of employee leaders it faces rather than by principle. When employee leaders were viewed as socialist radicals and charlatans, and it was thought that they would be thrown out of office if workers were given a chance to vote freely, management campaigned for government supervised voting by the rank-and-file. Now that the rank-and-file appear to be the radicals and many of their leaders somewhat more "realistic", the campaign is for a reversal to past practices. It is not clear whether management representatives appreciate fully the implications of the nature of authority that they wish to place in the hands of executives of employee organisations. Aside from the fact that a fundamental democratic principle would be violated, it is likely to increase conflicts within employee organisations, which will inevitably effect adversely the whole process of labour–management relations. The sort of legislation that is implied in the campaign is simply not possible in the current social and political environment. The refusal of employees to observe injunctions that they regard unjust, and the refusal to abide by orders of legislative assemblies to terminate strikes, provide some indication of the nature of response one would expect to legislation which would deprive them of the right to participate in the final determination of the terms and conditions of their employment.

Nevertheless, there have been occasions when management negotiators refused to negotiate allegedly because the employee negotiating committees did not have authority to conclude final agreements. Such approaches to bargaining are designed to score legal points, to place obstacles on the process, to delay; it is a sad manifestation of legal nonsense being allowed to over-ride common sense. There is no evidence that membership ratification is potentially an obstacle to the successful conclusion of agreements without undue delays and without interruptions in production processes. If occasionally a majority of members refuse to sanction an agreement recommended to them by their negotiating committee, that should be taken as a signal that something is wrong with the general state of relations between employees and management, between employees and leaders of their organisation, or that the lines of communication between employees and their bargaining committees are twisted. Rejection of a proposed agreement should never be interpreted to mean dissatisfaction with the agreement itself and nothing else. Such an interpretation will only invite repetition of the scenario next time around.

In the consideration of all issues related to ratification the question has arisen about alternatives to membership ratification without impeding the freedom of employee negotiating committees to carry out their responsibilities expeditiously and effectively. One such alternative would be to vest the authority for ratification to assemblies or councils of elected delegates. This will facilitate more effective communication from negotiating committees on the progress of negotiations, and will provide a better forum for discussion of proposed agreements than is possible at meetings of the membership at large. The present practice of calling mass meetings of the membership, frequently involving thousands of workers, is not appropriate for the effective presentation of contractual issues and their effective discussion.

4 The Wage and Salary Structure

In 1981, the weekly earnings of production workers in the United States averaged at around $255, giving an average annual income from full-time employment of $13 260: in service activities they averaged at about $209 per week, for an annual income from full-time employment of $10 868; whereas in construction the average was close to $400, for an annual income from employment of $20 800.[1] The same year, the Chief Executive Officer of W. R. Grace was paid a salary of $1 549 000; the Chief Executive Officer of ITT was paid $1 150 000; the Chief Executive Officer of EXXON was paid $1 105 412; and the Chief Officer of Sears Roebuck was paid $1 010 137. Boeing paid its Chief Executive $957 551; IBM paid $940 000; and General Electric $853 976.[2]

It is generally recognised that incomes will differ amongst occupations and employments. People differ in native abilities; the costs incurred in the acquisition of knowledge and skills vary; people bear different degrees of employment responsibilities and face different risks; some employments are more secure than other; people differ in the degree of effort they put forth in their work, which is reflected in the quantity and quality of their work; people differ in the values they put to work and leisure, to work environments, to regions and cities; and people differ in their preferences of the nature of work they wish to do. All of these differences and preferences can be expected to be reflected in differences in employment incomes.

But, while the differences and preferences provide economic rationale for differences in incomes from employment, they do not tell what the income differences should be: how much more or less should people earn for the things they do. The distribution of income from employment is a distribution of economic prizes to the participants in the economic process. The critical

53

question is the extent to which the prizes reflect the relative contributions of the participants to the output of the goods and services that have been produced. Do some participants get prizes that exceed their contributions? In such case, some other participants will get prizes that are lower than their contributions.[3]

There is widespread belief in society at large that differences in pay *from employment* do not reflect the differences in contributions people make in their employment activities: some occupations and employments earn considerably more than their contributions, while other earn considerably less. If this assertion is substantially correct, then the existing distribution of incomes from employment violates society's sense of equity, and means that society at large will support measures that promise a more equitable wage and salary structure.

But, while there may be general agreement that the pay structure is inequitable in relation to relative contributions, there is no social consensus on what differences in employment incomes should be amongst occupations and employments.[4] All kinds of variables influence the average citizen's concept of the relative worth of different occupations and employments, mostly subjective influences founded on social and personal value systems. Ask any diverse group of citizens to (a) *rank* the occupations listed in Table 4.1 in terms of the employment incomes they should receive – the highest (1), the second highest (2), the third highest (3), and so on; (b) indicate the *differences* in employment income that should exist amongst them – the highest ranked 300 per cent more than the lowest ranked, 250 per cent more than the second lowest, and so on; and (c) *justify* the suggested rankings and differences. The results will most surely be chaotic.

When the wage and salary structure is adjudged inequitable by citizens at large, yet there is no social consensus on what the structure should be, it is difficult for the public authority to establish corrective policy measures. It can be argued, of course, that if citizens at large have adjudged the structure inequitable, it is the responsibility of the public authority to identify the sources of inequity, and introduce measures to remove them or to remove their inequitable outcomes. For example, if the collective bargaining process were identified as a contributor to inequities in the wage structure, then a tax-based incomes policy[5] may be an effective approach to the restoration of equity. Similarly, if it should be established that the legal self-governance of some professions bestows monopoly powers on them which materialise in income inequities, appropriate amendments could be introduced to the relevant Acts to preclude such outcomes.

Equity is a troublesome issue in every society, regardless of economic, social and political structure. It is troublesome because it involves value judgements based on philosophy and self-interest. Unlike efficiency decisions, which concern the means used to achieve the ends of the economy (the organisation of production processes, and decisions on the nature and mix of factors of production), equity decisions concern the distribution of the ends of the economy – who should get what.[6]

Advocates of free market economies avoid the issue of equity by reference to the operation of market forces. Whatever the outcomes in the economy – unemployment or inequitable distribution of

TABLE 4.1   *Ranking occupations by employment incomes they 'should' earn*

Occupations	Rank	Differences (above & below Average)	Justifications
Lawyer			
High School Teacher			
Janitor			
Journalist			
Secretary/Typist			
Electrician			
Doctor			
Cashier in Grocery Store			
Postman			
Radio Announcer			
House Painter			
Engineer			
Auto Assembly Worker			
President of Large Company			
Insurance Salesman			
Steel Worker			
Garbage Collector			
Advertising Executive			
Member of Parliament			
Average Stage Actor			
Senior Government Bureaucrat			
Brewery Worker			
Nurse			

income – it is attributed to the free movement of factors, and free choices in the market place, which give expression to individual preferences. Hence whatever distribution in employment and output may emerge, it is deemed equitable in the context of the operation of a free market reflecting relative productivities, preferences relating to work and leisure, occupational preferences, industrial and geographic preferences relating to employment, and other individual decisions which bear on who gets what, who is employed and who is employed where.

But, are the choices free expressions of preferences? Are market outcomes the result of competitive forces or the result of monopolistic decisions? Furthermore, market determined distribution does not mean it is value-free distribution: whatever its nature, it will reflect some of the value judgements of the social and political system. *Value judgements have to enter the system at least once!*[7] The relative prizes attached to the services of refuse collectors, grave-diggers, physicians, electricians, management personnel, accountants, carpenters, teachers and nurses, manifest relative market forces as well as a certain social perception of the relative values of the respective occupations in our society.

Equity considerations would dictate the determination of whose value judgements are at the foundation of the distributive system. Historically they have been found to have emanated from dominant individuals, groups and institutions: the priest-kings in ancient Egypt and Babylonia; the Israelites through the Old Testament; the philosophers in Plato's City-States; the commercially-minded kings of Crete and Phoenicia; the Christian Church; the capitalist entrepreneurial class; the Marxists. The values that were given expression in writings and practices over the centuries constitute the foundation of our civilisation; the value judgements that we apply in the determination of economic prizes and social relationships are based largely on the teachings and practices of those groups.

The recognition that market determined distributions are not value-free, raises the question of criteria used in the determination of equity. What criteria should or can be used to determine whether a system of differential prizes is equitable or inequitable? The question is not whether differential prizes should exist; it is rather whether the existing differential standings are equitable or inequitable. There are many opinions on the issue, all of which manifest different values and different perceptions of the activities of occupations and individuals in society and the economy. We have not made any notable progress in the formulation of generally acceptable principles on the issue.[8]

CHANGES IN OCCUPATIONAL INCOME RELATIONSHIPS

Western societies are in the midst of a structural reorganisation. Existing social, occupational and income relationships are being re-examined and re-evaluated. There are indications that the end result of this re-examination will be a set of relationships quite different from the relationships in existence over the recent past.[9]

At present the re-examination is carried out largely in a vacuum: there is no evidence that it is based on any specific social, political or economic philosophies. Rather, it appears to have been initiated and sustained by a general view that existing social, occupational and income relationships cannot be justified on the basis of any generally acceptable economic and social grounds, and that, therefore, new sets of relationships must be found. The stratified ordering of occupational groups into unskilled labourers, semi-skilled operatives, skilled craftsmen, clerical, para-professional, technical, professional, managerial and administrative, and the direct association of that ordering with social status and employment income is being challenged. The question is being asked, what is a proper relationship between occupations, employments and incomes? What factors should be taken into account in determining the relationship?

Historically, inter-occupational wage comparisons were limited to skilled–unskilled differentials and to comparable occupations. A fundamental change has taken place in recent years: increasingly, references are made to the entire wage and salary structure, and comparisons are not limited to like with like; also, there is a general expectation that inter-occupational wage and salary differences will narrow, and that new relationships will emerge.

The evolution of new occupation-income relationships is, and will remain for some time, a major source of conflict in labour–management relations. A similar problem arose in the late 1940s and early 1950s with differences in wage rates between skilled and unskilled workers, which had narrowed significantly during the 1939–45 period of wartime regulation.[10] But conflicts were generally avoided because many of the skilled agreed not to resist the pressures on employers by the unions of the unskilled. Had the skilled insisted on the maintenance of traditional differentials, employers would have been confronted with leap-frogging demands for wage changes not unlike the ones they have faced in recent times.

The fundamental problem with changes in occupational wage and salary relationships is that it is difficult to justify them; and the difficulty arises from the fact that existing relationships are not based on any sets of clearly identifiable factors. As a result, when an occupational group demands increases in pay which appear excessive relative to what similarly placed occupational groups have received, it can argue that it does not recognise the existing relationships or that it regards traditional occupational comparisons inequitable. In the absence of specific wage determining criteria, which show why there are differences in pay between occupations, and why the differences are as wide as they are, it is not possible to determine whether demands for changes in relationships are justifiable. As long as there are no widespread demands for change, tradition remains the principal determining criterion. But, when groups begin to challenge the traditional relationships, and begin to jockey for new positions in the occupational and income scale, conflicts arise amongst occupational groups and between individual groups and management.

Understandably, governments are reluctant to become involved in disputes that arise from such inter-occupational pay conflicts. Involvement by the political process will, depending on the nature of involvement, provide a philosophical basis for existing or emerging wage and salary relationships. But, the political processes governing western nations do not have clearly delineated philosophies on which to base occupational income relationships. Even so-called Socialist governments, which profess commitment to the protection and advancement of the interests of "working people", have not come forth with propositions that manifest different sets of values and different work-income relationships than those in existence. Compulsory arbitration, too, is unlikely to bring about acceptable new relationships. As indicated above, it is as difficult to find justifications for departures as it is to find justifications for what exists.

Two hundred years ago, Adam Smith suggested five principal factors that influence inter-occupational wage relationships in a competitive market:

> First, the wages of labour vary with the ease or hardship, the cleanliness or dirtiness, the honourableness or dishonourableness of the employment.
>
> Secondly, the wages of labour vary with the easiness and cheapness, or the difficulty and expense of learning the business. . . . A man educated at the expense of much labour and time to any of those employments that require extraordinary dexterity and skill, . . . (the income) will replace to him the whole expense of his education, with at least the ordinary profits of an equally valuable capital. . . . The difference between wages of skilled labour and those of common labour is founded upon this principle. . . . Education in the ingenious arts and in liberal professions, is still more tedious and expensive. The pecuniary recompense, therefore, of painters and sculptors, of lawyers and physicians, ought to be much more liberal: and it is so accordingly.
>
> Thirdly, the wages of labour in different occupations vary with the constancy or inconstancy of employment. . . . In the greater part of manufactures, a journeyman may be pretty sure of employment almost every day in the year that he is able to work. A mason or bricklayer, on the contrary, can work neither in hard frost nor in foul weather . . . the high wages (of building) workers, therefore, are not so much the recompense of their skill, as the compensation for the inconstancy of their employment.
>
> Fourthly, the wages of labour vary according to the small or great trust which must be reposed in the worker. The wages of goldsmiths and jewellers are everywhere superior to those of many other workmen . . . on account of the precious materials with which they are entrusted. We trust our health to the physician; our fortune and sometimes our life and reputation to the lawyer and attorney. . . . Their reward must be such, therefore, as may give them that rank in the society which so important a trust requires.
>
> Fifthly, the wages of labour in different employments vary according to the probability or improbability of success in

them. . . . In a profession where twenty fail for one that succeeds, that one ought to gain all that should have been gained by the unsuccessful twenty.[11]

It is important to note that none of these five factors taken by itself is adequate for the determination of an appropriate wage: some of the factors are complementary to one another, and some offset each other. For example, the physician's work is relatively hard; the period of study required of physicians is relatively long, hard and expensive; and the trust reposed in physicians is considerable. All these would justify a relatively high wage. But, on the other hand, the occupation is an honourable one; employment is secure; and artificially maintained scarcity has raised the probability of success in practice above that of many other employments. These should have a downward effect on the wages of physicians. Furthermore, increasingly most of the direct cost of their education and training is borne by society. This too, should have a downward effect on their wages. Another appropriate example is the policeman: the work is also hard; it is equally unpleasant at times; considerable trust is reposed in the policeman; the work is relatively dangerous; and the probability of success in the occupation is relatively low. All these would justify a relatively high wage. But, the period of training is relatively short; there are no educational and training expenses; there is employment security; and there does not appear to exist any scarcity of people with the educational and personal qualifications required of prospective policemen. These have a downward effect on the policeman's wage. The actual wage that will be earned in a competitive market will be the wage that will emerge on balance from these opposing factors. But, that would not resolve our problem: on balance the factors tell us why there are differences and why there should be differences in wages and salaries amongst occupations; they do not tell us how wide the differences ought to be. Conflicts over increases in wages and salaries relate largely to this issue.

The substance of this proposition is that most conflicts over wages and salaries are conflicts over the distribution of wages, salaries and other forms of employment income. Traditionally leaders of organised labour have argued that pay-related conflicts are over the distribution of national income between wages and profits; and some still do. But, those who do are either ignorant of the real situation or are politically motivated. The share of national income taken into profit, and retained by the owners of capital, is so small as to make little difference to the general level of wages and salaries even if it were transferred into them in its entirety. When account is taken of the proportion of profits taken by governments, and the proportion reinvested in production processes – two kinds of allocation that will continue regardless whether enterprises are privately or publically owned – what remains can hardly be an issue in the determination of wage policy. It is the distribution of employment income amongst participants in economic, social and political activity that is the source of controversy and conflict; not the distribution of national income between wages and profits.

INTER-OCCUPATIONAL CONFLICTS OVER THE BUSINESS CYCLE

Inter-occupational conflicts become particularly intensive during periods of no-growth. When growth is rapid, all claims to the increment in goods and services can more or less be accommodated – some more, some less on each round, but nevertheless some improvements in living standards are achieved and conflicts are minimised. Problems arise when periods of no-growth set in: at such times, commitments made to various groups during the period of growth cannot be satisfied without imposing sacrifices on other groups; conflicts arise with key groups in the occupational structure determined to maintain their relative income positions; and the expectations of groups left behind during periods of growth cannot be fulfilled without sacrifices by groups which gained substantially. Therefore, although it appears on the surface as if conflicts are between those who pay the wages, salaries, fees, commissions, and other forms of employment income and those who receive them, in reality most conflicts are conflicts amongst occupational groups over the distribution of income amongst them. Quest for more from an unchanged quantity means more to some less to others. Those who seek more on such occasions should be asked to indicate whose incomes should be reduced so that they can be given more.[12]

In periods of growth, the strongly organised, the dominant occupations in production processes, and managerial (administrative) decision-makers allow improvements in the relative income positions of the low-paid because the sacrifice on themselves is relatively small. Indeed, the extent of improvements that they allow is frequently determined by the degree of sacrifice that they themselves are willing to bear. There is no other rational explanation for the wide differences in pay between men and women, between professional occupations and the scores of non-professionals working with them, between the strongly organised and the unorganised or ineffectively organised. In a free market the forces of demand and supply will set the differences; but, in a market whose processes are dominated by the organised, the professional and technical, and by various managerial (administrative) groups, what the low-paid get is determined by what sacrifices these groups are willing to make.

As indicated above, the influence of these dominant groups does not manifest itself in periods of growth because at such periods they suffer relatively small sacrifices from the improvements in the relative income positions of the low-paid. It manifests itself in periods of no-growth, when any real improvements in the relative income positions of the low-paid is likely to be at their expense. Witness, for example, the conflicts in recent years between relatively low-paid civil servants and the civil service bureaucracy; between the high-paid administrators and professionals who control and administer autonomously governed public and semi-public institutions, such as hospitals and educational institutions, and the mass of low-paid workers employed in them; witness the resistance to the long overdue improvements in the relative income positions of women in the labour force; and witness the resistance of middle-management groups, who themselves aspire to promotions with substantial increases in pay, to significant improvements in the relative income positions of the low-paid. These are inter-occupational conflicts, between the relatively high-paid and the low-paid, over the distribution of employment income in periods of no-growth; they are not conflicts between owners of capital and wage-earners over the distribution of income between wages and profits.

IN SEARCH OF SOLUTIONS

What implications are suggested by these conflicts? When capital was central in the economic process, and its ownership was clearly identified with individuals or families, it was relatively easy to determine whether the owner–capitalist was taking out of the process too much for himself and allocating too little to those employed in the production process. Now that the occupational mix of the labour force has become very diverse, and the place of the capitalist–owner–manager has been taken by a multitude of managers and professional specialists, income allocation amongst occupations has become the difference that divides. Who is to be the arbiter in this new system? It cannot be the political process, since it is devoid of philosophy, and cannot provide a political set of inter-occupational wage relationships; it cannot be the market, since market forces are influenced by organisational, legislative, administrative and institutional regulations that favour individual occupational groups; and it cannot be the collective bargaining process, since not all of the working population are organised for collective bargaining purposes.

Two developments are critical to the evolution of an equitable pay structure: one is the establishment of greater social consensus on equity in inter-occupational pay relationships, and the other is the establishment of a politically independent institutional arbiter to monitor changes, and make pronouncements on developments that are likely to have distortive consequences.

Social consensus on equity in inter-occupational pay relationships can only evolve from the employment environment itself; it cannot be imposed by some political or social authority. Any authority external to the employment process, regardless how socially representative in its composition, will be attributed values and influences alien to the realities of the employment relationships, environments and processes. Workers tend to the view that they themselves are better qualified to assess the relative values of the work performed by their co-workers. Given the opportunity to bargain amongst themselves, they are likely to evolve more acceptable, more equitable and more enduring inter-occupational pay structures than those formulated by the wage and salary administration offices of enterprises. An assertion was made elsewhere in this chapter that if a diverse group of people were to rank occupations and assign relative values, the result would be chaotic. It is asserted here that if the diverse group were constituted of the occupations themselves, a different order would emerge. The public at large has a different perception of employment relationships and relative values of work than do those involved in the work processes. The test of this hypothesis will be in the results from a diverse group of citizens ranking and evaluating the occupations in Table 4.1, and the occupations themselves carrying out the same exercise.

This proposition suggests that social consensus on equity can best evolve from consensus amongst employees on the relative values of the work performed by them. The process by which such consensus can evolve would be by a system of bargaining which involves all occupations employed by each enterprise together. The existing system in which some occupations bargain together, some bargain individually, and some do not bargain at all, precludes the possibility of consensus evolution through inter-occupational discussion and bargaining. If all occupational groups employed by individual enterprises were required to bargain jointly, the battleground over inter-occupational differences will shift from the bargaining table to the joint multi-occupational negotiating committees. Each occupational group would be compelled to justify to the other groups the rate of pay that it seeks for itself, before the issue is taken to the bargaining table. For example, if teachers, custodians, secretaries and other occupational groups employed by boards of education were to be required to prepare jointly the package of terms and conditions of employment to be negotiated, and if doctors, nurses, physiotherapists, orderlies and other hospital workers were to be required to negotiate jointly with hospital boards, they would have to first agree amongst themselves who should get what for their services. The doctor would have to convince his co-workers that his services are worth four or five times on the average more than the average value of their services.

An instructive lesson on this issue is found in the conflicts over wage differences between skilled and unskilled workers during the 1940s and early 1950s. It is an instructive lesson because the occupational relationship and social standing of the two groups was at that time somewhat the same as the relationship that exists today between the professional (including managerial and administrative) and all other occupational groups. The skilled regarded the unskilled as their helpers and insisted on wage differences that reflected that view. Differences of about 100 per cent between skilled and unskilled were a commonly recognised standard. The traditional explanation for the very wide differences was that there was a relative abundance of unskilled workers, that the skilled underwent a long apprenticeship period at relatively low apprentice pay, and that they had a social status to maintain. But, notwithstanding the validity of such explanations, the element that sustained the differences over time was the functional work relationship between the skilled and unskilled in the production process. As long as the functional role of the unskilled remained that of a helper to the skilled, the differences remained under the dictation of those whom they helped – the skilled.

In the late 1940s and early 1950s the unskilled began to assert themselves. They challenged the functional dependence relationship in the work process, demonstrated their independent functional roles, and challenged the skilled to justify their substantially higher wages. It did not take much pressure for the skilled to concede that perhaps the value of their work did not differ from the value of work of the unskilled to the extent of the differences in their pay. There followed then a succession of adjustments, which narrowed the differences to mutually acceptable levels. Arguments continue, of course, on whether existing differences reflect fully the relative contributions by the different categories of skilled and unskilled workers, but there appears to exist a general consensus within enterprises, at the managerial as well as the worker levels, that the differences are reasonably equitable. This cannot be said in relation to the prevailing differences amongst occupational groups generally – within the managerial/administrative structure, within professional groups, between professional groups, and among managerial, professional, para-professional, technical, office and other occupational groups.

Not unlike present-day arguments about "traditional" wage and salary relationships, the skilled regarded the pre-1939 differentials as fixed by tradition. But when pressed to justify them on the basis of the relative values of the services provided by themselves and the unskilled, they could not do so to anyone's satisfaction. Concerns were expressed about the effect that narrower differentials would have on the supply of skilled workers, but such concerns could not be supported by evidence that existing differentials were an important factor in individual decisions to enter educational and apprenticeship programmes which led to occupational specialisations and work-skills. This issue continues to cause concern. Management spokesmen have frequently expressed the view that the scarcity of some skilled occupations must be attributed largely to the lack of monetary incentives – too narrow a difference in pay between the skilled, the unskilled and the operatives. They also allege that the lack of "worthwhile" monetary incentives have made it increasingly difficult to attract competent individuals into middle-management positions. But, there is no evidence that inter-occupational wage and salary differences are an important factor in occupational choices: the levels of wages and salaries may be, but not necessarily the differences in wages and salaries between occupations. In other words, the salaries paid to teachers may influence the numbers that will go into the teaching profession; the difference in employment income between teaching and plumbing or carpentry will not necessarily influence the number that will enter and remain in teaching.

Another lesson provided by the skilled–unskilled differentials controversy of the 1940s and the 1950s is that the recognition by the skilled that the "traditional" gap between themselves and the unskilled may have been wider than what could be justified, and their acquiescence to search for more equitable or more acceptable differentials, prevented the emergence of leap-frogging increases in wages, which so frequently result from conflicts of that nature. Had the skilled insisted on the maintenance of the traditional differentials, a wage-cost spiral would have resulted, with serious implications for price stability. This lesson of the recent past provides two prescriptions for the current difficulties: one is that insistence on the maintenance of traditional differentials when lower-paid occupations attempt to improve their incomes results in leap-frogging, which has cost and price implications; and the other is that the avoidance of labour–management conflicts on the issue rests largely with the occupational groups which insist on the maintenance of traditional differentials. It is time that managerial, administrative, professional and technical occupations examine the relationship of their employment incomes (salaries, bonuses, commissions, fees, etc.) to the wages and salaries of other occupations and make an effort to justify them, or failing that to search for more equitable and more acceptable relationships. To the extent that existing relationships can be justified on the basis of economic criteria, such as scarcity in supply relative to demand and the consequent need to attract additional manpower into the relevant occupations, or the actual and imputed personal costs incurred in the acquisition of specific occupational skills, a rational argument can be made for their preservation;[13] but to the extent that they are founded on tradition or on some nebulous arguments, such as the preservation of the social standing of occupations, a search for more justifiable relationships would be warranted.

From a practical standpoint, the only effective way in which inter-occupational wage and salary relationships can be scrutinised is multi-occupational bargaining. As suggested above, if all occupations engaged in the production of given goods and services were to jointly prepare demands for changes in their conditions of employment, and were to thereby become compelled to justify to each other their wage and salary levels, continuous critical examinations of the relative differences would take place and appropriate adjustments would be instituted. The inter-occupational checks and balances that would result from such a procedure are more likely to find and sustain economically justifiable and socially acceptable differences in employment incomes amongst occupations, than can be established by the existing market, or by any boards, commissions and tribunals. The existing market is too imperfect; and the role of boards, commissions and tribunals should be to protect the public interest against collusive arrangements between employers and individual occupational groups, and to protect relatively weak occupational groups against exploitation by groups which command dominant positions in the organisational structures and work processes of enterprises and institutions.

MONITORING INSTITUTIONS AND AGENCIES

Recognition that the market is imperfect, which means, amongst other things, that it rewards excessively the strong and penalises excessively the weak, provides social justification for some kind of monitoring of the outcomes of bargains that go on in it all the time. In *laissez-faire* theory the market itself does the monitoring, and automatic market responses and adjustments take place to correct imperfections. In democratic political systems, governments and government agencies are presumed to be carrying out monitoring functions, and to establish game rules which ensure fair play. Our system is not *laissez-faire*, and governments are themselves major participants in market games. The outcomes of game plays cannot be expected to be fair to all when one of the interested parties sets the rules by which the games are to be played, acts as referee, and occasionally dictates the outcomes. When governments and government bureaucracies become players in the marketplace, in competition with non-government industrial, commercial and institutional enterprises, and the market is too imperfect to maintain effective checks and balances, it is in the interest of society at large that the monitoring function be vested in politically independent institutions and agencies. The media perform such a function to some extent, and so do independent researchers in universities, and consumer agencies. But, their effectiveness notwithstanding, their scope is necessarily limited. Government involvement is so widespread, collusive arrangements in business, between governments and business, between business and unions, so common, and the range of issues so vast, as to require continuous monitoring of the ways in which market games are played, and the outcomes of those games.

There is a need for politically independent institutions and agencies with powers to monitor changes in payments and make pronouncements on their relative merits. Given sets of wage and salary standards founded on generally acceptable economic and social criteria, the relevant institutions and agencies should be in a position to make effective pronouncements on both the increases in payments and the relative levels of wages and salaries. It is critical from the standpoint of effectiveness that the monitoring and related pronouncements cover all occupational and employment categories, relate to all payments, in whatever forms they are made, and apply to all enterprises, including governments and organisations. There should be no exceptions, particularly in relation to those at the bottom of the wage and salary scale, who are commonly victims of their weak competitive positions, in relation to those at the top of the income scale, who are commonly in position to dictate the payments for their services, and in relation to governments, which in quest of political self-interest are prone to violate all standards.

In such a setting, collective bargaining should flourish, unimpeded from governments, management or the union bureaucracy, and agreements will go unchallenged as long as the payment provisions can be justified on the basis of the generally recognised economic and social criteria. The same process would apply to payments that are not established through a collective bargaining process. Instances of collective and private agreements that depart from the generally accepted standards without acceptable justification, and instances of self-serving collusive arrangements between parties would invite public pronouncements by the relevant institutions and agencies, and where necessary, recommendation for corrective action by some appropriately designated enforcement agency. In this context, the monitoring institutions and agencies are conceived as instruments whose primary role would be to remove weaknesses and imperfections from the process of payments determination, so that a more just and equitable structure of employment income distribution will evolve.

THE PROBLEM OF ANNUAL INCREASES IN PAY

A serious problem in employer–employee relations is the practice, evolved over almost 35 years (1945–80) of continuous economic growth, of granting annual increases in pay. It should not surprise anyone that a practice of such long duration has become a custom, which like other customs demands observance, regardless of individual circumstances. An expectation has been created that pay will increase annually regardless of the employer's ability to pay. Custom dictates that the employer accommodate the expectation.

The accommodation of expectations for annual increments in pay when there are no increments in total revenue means, of course, that offsetting adjustments must take place in prices, employment, or both, and as well perhaps in the payments to the other factors that participate in the production of the output. All such forced adjustments are sources of conflict not only between the parties to the bargaining process, but also between them and the public at large: whether the outcome is increase in prices or decrease in employment,[14] the cost of the offsetting adjustment will fall in part on the public at large. In view of this, the parties to the bargaining process should be required in such instances to indicate publicly the nature of offsetting adjustments they would favour. It is conceivable that the bargaining process would improve if the parties were required to determine and make known to the public at large the possible offsetting adjustments that are related to the various hypothetical outcomes of their bargains.

The extent to which the practice of annual increases in pay has become a custom is manifested in the following communication from a union to its members:

> The postwar era saw a lengthy period of industry expansion, with lower rates, high profits, and rising wages. Labour relations was confined to the simple matter of distributing the growing wealth. As long as the happy combination endured, we were little inclined to quarrel with the managers who claimed responsibility for the miracle ... that golden age came to a sudden end a few years ago. What do we see now? Rate increases every year, and falling profits. The result, inevitably, is a massive assault on employees' interests, as management vainly seeks a return to the golden age.[15]

The "massive assault on employees' interests" was in management efforts to increase productivity through technological changes, which impacted on work activities, required retraining and relocation, and in increases in wages that were lower than the increases to which they had become accustomed.

The reality of the relationship between the value of output and the shares of it going to the factors that participate in its production, dictates that increments in factor payments be related to the increments in the value of output.[16] It should be recognised that changing market conditions for factors may dictate from time to time that increments to individual factors of production be higher than the increment in the value of output, in which case increments to the other factors will have to be lower. The practice of demanding and granting increments that are not related to the increment in the value of output, and forcing thereby offsetting adjustments in prices and employment cannot be beneficial in the long run to the economy at large or to employment. Increases in prices weaken the competitive position of enterprises, with negative effects on demand, particularly for enterprises which compete with foreign products; and the increasing cost of labour compels enterprises to search for processes which use less labour. The saving of labour when the labour force is expanding means unemployment.

The custom of annual increments in pay regardless of the capacity of enterprises and the economy to pay must give away to the reality of the relationship between the value of output and payments to the factors involved in its production. The custom-founded attitude of most employees and leaders of employee organisations that they do not care where the funds will be found for increments in pay, must give away to the reality that "finding" the funds may result in negative effects on employment and on living standards through inflation. Individual enterprises may be able to carry the burden of increments in pay that exceed the increment in the value of output one or two years, as many have had to do frequently, but when such practice persists over prolonged periods of time, and when it occurs in periods of decline in activity, the cumulative cost-effects usually result in drastic adjustments in production processes. Over time such adjustments have invariably meant less employment: which means in effect that the rising standard of living of those who persist in demands for higher pay regardless of the capacity of enterprises to pay, is at the cost of those who find employment in those enterprises progressively diminishing.

THE WORK ENVIRONMENT AS A CONTRIBUTING FACTOR

It is conceivable, of course, that the indicated attitude of employees and leaders of employee organisations is a manifestation of doubt in the veracity of managerial pronouncements, and a reaction to the work environment. A question of considerable consequence for employer–employee relations, is the extent to which the customs, practices and standards that have evolved over time are a response to the adversarial relationships that are found in most enterprises. If this should be the case, then the question would arise whether such customs, practices, and standards will be modified in a system of relationships which provides for greater participation by workers in decision-making on issues that relate directly to the ways in which they perform their work functions and to the work environments in which they labour. Would workers trade-off their quest for annual increases in their pay, regardless of capacity to pay, for a work environment in which they feel a part, and from which they derive satisfaction? There is utility in the performance of meaningful work, and in the knowledge that the work environment can be changed to accommodate changing social conditions in the workplace. It can reasonably be expected, therefore, that given worker participation in the design of work processes and work organisation, and given an effective means of worker participation in the formulation of rules and regulations that govern the work environment, relations between employees and management can be expected to improve, which is a prerequisite to the evolution of mutual trust, and which in turn is a condition for any substantive change in the attitudes and expectations of employees.[17] When a job offers nothing more than the earning of an income, it will be treated as such – the job to be done as well as it can be done with the minimum of effort, for an income that is to rise in direct relation to the dissatisfaction that the job yields. On the other hand, when the job offers more than income, when it offers a social environment from which the employee derives satisfaction, and when the work itself provides personal fulfillment, the attitudes of employees towards their jobs can be expected to be positive, which will inevitably be reflected in their expectations.[18] It can reasonably be expected that the quest for more will not be a priority expectation at all times, and that their expectations will reflect the reality of the level of activity and the capacity to pay. Indeed, it can be asserted that improvements in the social environment of the workplace and personal fulfillment from work will increase productivity, which will improve the capacity to pay, and thereby provide increasing incomes.[19] Which suggests that improvements in the social environment of the workplace, and changes in the organisation of work designed to generate personal fulfillment to those performing the work, should not be viewed as costly undertakings to be offset by reductions in increments of pay. They should be viewed rather as positive undertakings, with potentially positive effects on productivity, and therefore, positive effect on incomes.[20]

5 Patterns of Wage Bargaining and Wage Regulations

INTRODUCTION

In recent years, the unions of some key enterprises in the United States conceded reductions in contracted increases in pay, and initiated thereby discussions amongst industrial relations practitioners on whether such concessions have established a new pattern of wage bargaining.[1]

Three modes of pattern bargaining have been identified:[2] *intra-industry* wage followership, "where the settlement of one company is copied by other employers in the same industry"; *inter-industry* patterns, "where wage increases negotiated in one industry influence settlements in related industries"; and *the spill-over* effect, whereby union wage patterns "spill over and influence the *non-union* sectors as well".

In the case of the *intra-industry* pattern, the contract of the pattern-setting company usually becomes the "master" contract for all bargaining units affiliated with the company, and sets a standard in all of the labour markets in which the company has bargaining units. Commonly, local labour market conditions and distinctive characteristics of individual plants and operations have not been allowed to influence wage rates. Their influence has been limited to the multitude of local–specific non-wage terms and conditions of employment.

Concession bargaining is not new. It is a common form of bargaining in times of crisis. It will be found in varying degrees whenever *prolonged* declines in economic activity effected seriously the performance of individual enterprises and industries, and whenever unanticipated market changes reduced permanently the abilities of enterprises to pay. It would be misleading to interpret recent concessions as a reversal of long-standing

73

practices, and the establishment of a new trend in wage bargaining. Similar concessions have been recorded in other periods of economic decline, which lasted only as long as adverse economic conditions dictated.[3]

To management, concession bargaining is critical when profits decline substantially, and persist at low levels over prolonged periods. To employees and their leaders, concession bargaining can only be justified when there is evidence of difficulties which suggest the possibility of bankruptcy. A decrease in profits, regardless of the magnitude of the decrease, does not signal in itself difficulties that can be resolved by decreases in wages and other labour costs. There are many variables that bear on profits, including management competence. Concessions by employees will not necessarily correct the problems. Even when the problems can be identified as related to rates of pay relative to the rates prevailing in foreign competitive enterprises, a common reference in recent years, more effective corrective measures will be found in product designs, product quality and overall efficiency in the enterprise, than in reductions in rates of pay. Many more enterprises have been turned from unprofitable to profitable by changes in management than by reductions in pay and reductions in rates of increase in pay. Which suggests that more solutions to problems will be found in the nature and structure of management, than in the terms and conditions of employment of the work force. Wage concessions should be viewed as short-term relief, not as a corrective measure for industrial maladies the result of inefficiency, and products which cannot compete in international markets.

In cases of imminent bankruptcy, the question arises whether concessions by workers will forestall bankruptcy. It is to be expected that workers would wish to have evidence to that effect. Given such evidence, leaders of employee organisations should not encounter much opposition from the membership. Uncertainty is the most common cause of opposition in such instances: is the enterprise really in trouble or does management claim so to get concessions; will concessions by employees contribute significantly to the resolution of the problems; will the concessions be restored when profitability is restored; is there evidence of concessions on the part of all persons involved in the enterprise – management, shareholders, and suppliers of services to the enterprise, particularly suppliers with subsidiary corporate relationships. To answer these and related questions, leaders of employee organisations will have to be provided with information which enterprises have been reluctant to provide. Yet, without answers to such questions, leaders of employee organisations cannot enter into negotiations and reach agreement on concessions without risking rejection of both the agreements and themselves.

Unions must realise, of course, that companies that are giants within their domestic market, with characteristics that suggest ability to influence the market prices of their products, may be mere pygmies within the international market, compelled to accept the prices that are set by the market. In the context of the domestic market, they may appear able to transfer increases in wages into higher prices; in the context of the international market, and the competitive forces that they encounter in them, they may be forced to reduce their prices. Protection of the domestic market may enable such companies to transfer higher wages into higher prices, but to the extent that the operations of such companies are related to both the domestic and foreign markets, they may lose their foreign markets, and thereby lose the employment that is related to production for foreign markets. Furthermore, account must be taken of the response of demand in the home market to the increase in price. Demand may fall and cause further reductions in employment.

The important question for the future is whether the trade-off of wage concessions for employment in critical cases can become widespread when employment becomes threatened not by what is viewed as temporary decreases in demand, as in the automobile industry, for example, but by general structural and technological changes. Could acceptance of the principle of trade-off between employment and wages lead to a system of guaranteed employment? Heretofore, organised labour has tended to view wages as the dominant variable and employment as the adjusting variable in response to increases in wages. In other words, organised labour accepted the possibility that the increases in wages it sought may cause decreases in employment. The question now arises whether the isolated instances of trade-off of wages for employment will make employment the dominant variable and wages the adjusting variable. Is it possible that a certain portion of the wage, as in the case of the semi-annual bonus paid to workers in Japan, will, become the adjusting variable that will guarantee employment. In such case, wage concessions in the form of adjustments to the variable portion of the wage package, may become a permanent feature of wage bargaining.

THE JOB SECURITY ISSUE

Job security has not been a priority issue in the bargaining agendas of employee organisations. Claims to the contrary notwithstanding, there is little evidence of demonstrated readiness to forego increases in wages, accept decreases in wages or agree to decreases in hours of work for employment stability. The reduction in hours has been suggested occasionally as a remedy to unemployment, but it has always been made conditional on "no reductions in pay", which means in effect conditional on the introduction of offsetting increases in the hourly rates of pay.

It should not be surprising, of course, that job security should rank low with employee organisations: their policies reflect the will of the majority, and the majority is not usually affected by work force reductions. Even when economic conditions are most adverse, and the rate of unemployment increases, the numbers effected by layoffs and dismissals are relatively small. Most employees have de facto guaranteed employment.[4] The question is, then, whether the majority, which may be 70, 80, or 90 per cent of the work force, would be willing to suffer reductions in pay to save the jobs of the few. The self-interest of the majority has tended to prevail.

As long as changes in the economy at large and in the structure of industry affect the employment of relatively small proportions of the work force, employment security will remain an issue of low priority with employee organisations. Efforts will likely focus on the provision of income security during the periods of unemployment, with the burden of income security falling on the enterprises and governments, not on employee organisations and their employed members. But, there are strong indications that changes in the structure of industry, and changes in production processes, have begun to affect increasing

proportions of the work force. Yet, leaders of employee organisations have given no indication of policy changes which would
address this issue. It is conceivable that upon addressing the
issue they will conclude that nothing should be done – that
changes in technology and in the structure of industry, dictate
changes in occupations and employment, and that the cost of job
security in reduced productivity, and possibly fewer hours of
work with corresponding reductions in pay, will be more negative to labour at large than the cost of insecurity reflected in the
loss of employment. Evidence from countries, such as Japan,
where employment security is guaranteed in many enterprises
suggests no such costs from employment security either to the
economy and the enterprises or to employees at large.[5] Yet, it
must be recognised that what is practiced successfully in Japan
is not necessarily exportable to other countries.

Developments in technology, and the resultant changes in the
industrial structures of economies and in production processes
will compel employee organisations to take up the issue of
employment security. The outcome cannot be foretold: but, it is
unlikely that employee organisations and the majority of their
members who will continue to hold jobs of one sort or another
will agree to sacrifices that may promise continuing employment
to the minority. Instead, they will continue to demand of governments policies that would ensure full employment, and adequate
incomes to those who cannot be guaranteed employment. Which
means in essence that employee organisations and the majority
of their members will continue to demand that the cost of job
security be borne by society at large, not by themselves.

Such a response should not be surprising in the context of the
economic and political realities of most developed industrial
economies: organisations formed for the sole purpose of advanc-
ing the self-interest of their members can be expected to seek the
enhancement of their self-interest at cost to someone else. This is
as much the case with employee organisations as it is the case
with industry groups seeking tariff protection, or business groups
seeking reductions in business taxes. They accept the reality of
change, which is manifested in voluntary and involuntary exits
of members from their organisations, and concentrate their
efforts to the protection and enhancement of the interests of those
members who remain in their organisations.

WAGE STANDARD AND EMPLOYMENT

If employment for all were a priority goal, then the wage bill will have to be shared amongst all, which means the available work will have to be shared. The wages of all will have to drop proportionately. The idea that wages must rise regardless whether activity in the enterprise is constant, rising or falling is irrational and costly to workers. If workers deem it undesirable to have their wages fluctuating in line with the performance of the enterprises that employ them, then they should agree on some average wage standard, which will remain relatively fixed over time, and negotiate an increment that will fluctuate in line with some variable or variables, such as output or total revenue.[6] Profit is often used as a variable, but since workers and their organisations have no say on non-wage costs, do not influence total efficiency, including management efficiency, and do not participate in price determination and marketing, profits may not reflect the efforts and productivity of workers. Workers should not be penalised for mis-management, and they should not subsidise incompetent management. Therefore, the variable that will reflect worker effort is output; and it is output to which increments in pay should be related. Proportionate changes in output and increments in pay would establish a reasonably fair relationship between the state of the economy, the state of the enterprise and the workers' pay. Over time, as production processes change, price structures change, capital-labour ratios change, and labour-output ratios change, the wage standard can be adjusted to reflect the new realities. The pay packets of Japanese workers vary by as much as 30 per cent from one year to the next, depending on the size of bonuses they receive, which make up as much as 40 per cent of their total wage income. Their basic wage rates remain stable; and their employment remains secure. They share in the prosperity of their companies through the bonus system, and they suffer reductions in their bonuses in periods of adversity. *Variations in the size of bonuses are the employment stabiliser.* But, in many Japanese enterprises the human factor is deemed as fixed in the production process as is the capital factor. To the extent that society deems this to be desirable then adjustment mechanisms would have to be established which will guarantee employment.

Daniel Mitchell has suggested a system of "gain-sharing"

based on sales, production, productivity or revenue. Since these variables "are all heavily influenced by aggregate demand", the establishment of some relationship between them and increments in pay will make labour compensation "sensitive to the ups and downs of the business cycle".[7]

GAIN-SHARING AND INCOMES POLICY

Gain-sharing is the closest one can get to pay-setting behaviour that would parallel the state of economic conditions, and may be regarded as the most effective alternative to an incomes policy for highly decentralised labour and product markets where the enforcement of incomes policies is very difficult.[8]

Effective implementation of incomes policies is conditional on a significant degree of centralisation in decision-making on both terms and conditions of employment and pricing policies. Hence the effectiveness of incomes policies in some European countries, such as Austria and Sweden. In North America, decision-making is highly decentralised on both sides: neither major labour organisations nor management organisations have the authority, social, economic or political standing in the community at large, widespread support from their constituent parts, allegiance or whatever it takes to bring together, coordinate and influence the multitude of decision-making bodies. Economies with widely decentralised decision-making processes will be better served by gain-sharing systems.

The widespread existence of gain-sharing agreements can approximate the conditions of an incomes policy. To the extent that an effective incomes policy reflects the state of the economy, the widespread existence of gain-sharing agreements will, too, reflect the state of the economy: when the rate of economic activity increases, and output and profits increase the increment in income shares will increase; on the other hand, when the rate of economic activity decreases, and output and profits decrease, the increment in shares will fall. In other words, the increments in pay will become more sensitive to economic conditions than they have been heretofore.

There are problems, of course, with the system, which have arrested its introduction: one of these, to which reference was made above, concerns the responsibility workers should bear for inefficient management of enterprises. Reductions in gains the result of general decline in economic activity can be accepted; but, should workers be made to accept reductions that are the result of management inefficiency? The other problem is related to the sensitivity of prices to declines in the rate of economic activity. The behaviour of many prices and taxes has tended to be counter-cyclical in periods of decline in economic activity and pro-cyclical in periods of expansion; and the same can be said about such monopolistically determined charges as medical and dental, insurance rates, and interest rates. How can wage and salary earners be expected to respond in accordance with the signals and requirements of the economy, when the prices of goods and services that absorb most of their incomes are not equally sensitive? Unless suitable institutional arrangements can be made, which promise appropriate responses to changing economic conditions from all segments of the economy and society, including governments, professional practitioners, institutions, commercial organisations, and boards vested with powers to set rates and charges, it could not be expected that organisations of employees would acquiesce to arrangements that would make the increments in pay sensitive to prevailing or anticipated economic conditions.

PATTERN BARGAINING[9]

In the past three decades there evolved in North America a system of pattern bargaining within broad inter-related industrial sectors: a major agreement by one company generally established the guidelines for all other companies in the industry, particularly in relation to the wage increase. Recognition of the established standard, regardless of the state of the labour market, and regardless of abilities of individual companies to bear equal burdens, was based generally on "fairness". The argument was that if companies have the same or similar production processes, produce the same or similar products, and employ the same or similar workers, then different abilities to pay manifest differences in managerial abilities. In such cases, to ask workers to accept different rates of pay, would constitute subsidisation of management incompetence. By insisting on the same pay for the same work, workers would in effect ensure the existence of competition in the managerial hierarchy and the weeding out of the incompetent managers.

In addition to the sense of fairness, pattern bargaining has established itself firmly in North America because of the increasing role of the legal profession in negotiations. The legal profession is accustomed to the following of established precedents. That is the fundamental nature of its training. Departure from established precedents is commonly very slow, and requires significant changes in the premises on which the precedents are based.

Pattern bargaining is founded on two positive principles: one is the principle of "fairness", which postulates that it is only fair that workers similarly employed, in similar market conditions should receive similar adjustments in their wages; and the other is the principle of "ability to pay", and management responsibility for it. The first principle recognises that labour market conditions and the circumstances of individual enterprises may warrant increases greater or smaller than the established pattern during a given period, but it also recognises that during another period labour market conditions and circumstances of individual enterprises may change, and warrant greater or smaller increases to other workers. Over time *fairness* will tend to spread and equalise.

In relation to the issue of the ability of enterprises within a given industry to pay the same wages, the question arises whether workers should bear any part of the costs of management incompetence. Differences in ability to pay by the different enterprises in the automobile industry, for example, cannot be attributed to any differences in the skills and abilities of the workers since the workers are perfectly substitutable within the industry; differences in ability to pay must be attributed to the skills, abilities and decisions of management. To accept different wage rates and different increases in wages because of differences in ability to pay, will constitute subsidisation of managerial inefficiencies. Subsidisation breeds inefficiency; and as such it is not a rational solution to the problem of inefficiency. The rational solution to the problem of inefficiency is to remove the sources of inefficiency. To the extent that the sources are at the managerial hierarchy, acceptance of differences in pay increases would undermine the competitive process and delay the weeding out of the incompetents. Recent history records such developments in the automobile industry and the farm implements industry.

The same issue arises in relation to patterns of collective bargaining and government policies. Should the results of collective bargaining be in line with the requirements of government policies? Should unions tailor their wage demands in accordance with prevailing government policies, and should management pursue wage policies supportive of government policies? Accommodative responses would constitute implicit agreement with government policies. Yet, the record will show that oftentimes the policies pursued by governments are motivated by political self-interest which is not necessarily in the interest of either labour or management. Similarly, account must be taken of government incompetence, which if accommodated through "socially responsive bargaining"[10] may create economic difficulties. Socially responsive bargaining is based on the premise that government policies are socially responsible. The records of government policies, particularly those in effect during the late 1970s and early 1980s, cast considerable doubt on that premise. Labour and management cooperation with an incompetent government would constitute support of incompetence leading to survival, in the same way as union cooperation with incompetent management would constitute subsidisation and survival of incompetent management.

WAGE INSENSITIVITY

There is an important negative aspect to pattern bargaining: it is the disregard of changes in labour market conditions and changes in economic conditions generally. There would be no problem if all contracts had the same starting dates and the same duration. Then the same labour market conditions and the same general economic conditions would prevail for all. But, contracts are negotiated over different periods and have different starting and termination dates; and the labour market, and general economic conditions change over time. The labour market and general economic conditions that provide economic rationale for an agreement at a given period of time, may no longer provide such rationale six months later. Yet, the establishment and acceptance of pattern bargaining as a standard dictates the application of the agreed upon increases. This gives the impression of *wage insensitivity* to changing labour market and general economic conditions,[11] and the further impression of conscious decisions on the part of union leaders to trade-off the employment of some of their members for higher wages to those members who retain their employment.

The apparent insensitivity of union leaders to negative changes in economic conditions should not be attributed to any conscious quest for higher wages regardless of the effect on employment. The approach is dictated by an established practice which they cannot themselves break. The expectations of their members compel the practice, and dictate adherence to established principles. But, it is most unlikely that many of them would engage in militant action if a neutral authority, such as an arbitrator, were to call attention to changed labour market conditions and deterioration in the economy at large, and were to recommend a temporary departure from the established practice. In such instances labour leaders often seek a way out of the dictates of custom and established practices, and rely on neutral agents – arbitrators and even governments – to provide them. Understandably, they would expect justifications acceptable to those of their members who will be denied the increases given to their counterparts a few months earlier, and would expect some commitment that the "unfair" treatment will be corrected when labour market conditions and the economy show signs of improvement. Only a neutral arbitrator, respected by both management and the unions, and vested with powers to make conditional awards, can make departures from recognised practices acceptable. The acceptance of conditional departures depends on the confidence that the conditions will be put into effect when circumstances permit; which in turn depends on the reputation of the arbitrator and the trust of the parties in the arbitration process.[12]

The imposition by governments of standards, guidelines and controls which depart from established patterns and practices, and thereby effect some workers unfairly, without any commitment that the unfair treatment will be rectified at the first favourable opportunity, places union leaders in untenable positions: even though they may realise that circumstances dictate a break with established practices, they cannot express support for policies that are discriminatory in the context of established practices, unless acceptable justification is provided for temporary discrimination. Public authorities do not arbitrate individual cases the way arbitrators do; and as a result, cannot identify unfair effects on individual groups of workers, which would require rectification. The effect of controls is commonly more universal than arbitration decisions, and in their universatility they are frequently more discriminatory than the awards of arbitrators. A good arbitration system, with arbitrators who are not committed by custom, practice and training to apply precedents blindly, can be significantly less unfair to individual groups of workers, and substantially more efficient in terms of the maintenance of proper relationships between increases in wages and the state of the labour market and the economy, than the periodic imposition of controls and guidelines by governments.

THEORY OF EMPLOYMENT

Employment theory is based on the general principle that an employer will take on additional workers as long as the anticipated return from each of them exceeds the cost of their employment. The taking on of additional workers will stop when the return equals the cost. Variations about the equilibrium can be tolerated in the short run, as when an employer retains skilled workers in a slump so that they will be available in the upturn, and it is recognised that in family enterprises increasing family sizes may result in zero or negative contributions by individual family members, but these are exceptions. As a general rule increments to the value of output relative to increments in cost will determine the level of employment.

The problem with this general principle is that its application is limited to processes producing goods and services for the market place or goods and services that are subjected to market tests; and the other is the problem of identifying and measuring the contribution to the value of output of individual workers and even groups of workers. In public sector employments – government, education, health – and employments in organisations such as churches, trade unions, political parties, charitable enterprises and commercial clubs, contributions to the value of output cannot be determined, since the services that are being produced have no market price. Payments for such employments are largely based on comparative wage and salary criteria, which take into account the nature of the employments, degrees of responsibility, the state of demand and supply for the occupation, and such other, and employment is determined by their budgets, which means, the financial resources available to them.

It is noteworthy that equilibrium cannot be established in such employments, since only one side of the equation is available, namely, the cost side. The value added side is missing, even though within each process of each enterprise criteria exist on relative contributions of individual employees, which are used in the determination of promotions, increments in pay and other awards. But such valuations measure differences in efficiency and effectiveness in work performance amongst individual employees, not the additions to the total value of output. Therefore, employment in activities which do not produce for the market, and are not subjected to market tests, will be determined by budgets and ability to pay.[13]

WAGE INCREASES IN PERIODS OF UNEMPLOYMENT

Union leaders and some labour economists often present the aggregate demand argument in support of demands for increases in wages during periods of decline in economic activity and excess involuntary unemployment. The argument is that since production is related to aggregate demand, and effective aggregate demand is related to spending, increases in income will, other things being equal, increase aggregate demand, which in turn will increase production and employment.[14] This argument is fundamentally correct, other things being equal. What makes it incorrect are the "other things", which are not "equal", do not remain constant, and often neutralise the possible benefits of the increase in wages. One of the "other things" is productivity: wages and the wage bill are not wage costs; wage costs are determined by the ratio of the wage bill to output. Which means that if output increases faster than the increase in the wage bill, wage costs will decrease regardless how high wage rates might be; and conversely, if output were to increase slower than the increase in the wage bill, wage costs will increase, regardless whether the wage rates are high or low. This reality tells us that an increase in wages and in the wage bill (which is conditional on the increase in wages not being offset by a decrease in employment) without an increase in output, or with an increase in output by less than the increase in the wage bill, will increase wage costs.

Another of the "other things" is product prices: an increase in wage costs will dictate an increase in product prices, unless excess profits had been made in which case the increase in wage costs could be accommodated through lower profits. But, if there is no possibility of such redistribution and an increase in prices becomes necessary, then depending on the nature of demand for the product demand may decrease. The outcome in relation to aggregate demand will then depend on what happens *on balance* between the increase in demand associated with the increase in wages and the decrease in demand associated with the increase in prices.

Yet another critical issue, which frequently gets lost during discussions, arguments and conflicts about wages, is the fact that the conflicts are over *increases* in wages, not attempts to *decrease* wages. The issue is by how much wages should increase, not whether they should increase or decrease. Therefore, it is not a question of aggregate demand decreasing if a wage increase were not granted, given stable prices, it is rather one of aggregate demand not increasing by as much as may result from the granting of the wage increase. When the issue is approached from this standpoint, the aggregate demand argument assumes different magnitudes: if an enterprise cannot grant an increase, but is compelled to do so, and takes the necessary funds from workers it lays-off, then the increase in wages will be at the expense of employment, and aggregate demand may not change, except perhaps by the unemployment insurance payments that will be collected by the unemployed workers. In reality, if aggregate consumer demand were an important consideration, then spreading the unchanged wage bill over all of the workers is more likely to sustain the aggregate demand than an agreement which would give more to some workers at the cost of the employment of others. Spreading the wage bill will probably result in an increase of the average propensity to consume of the workers involved and thereby increase aggregate demand.

RESPONSIVENESS TO MARKET CONDITIONS

An issue of considerable consequence to the bargaining process is the response of employee organisations and management to

changing market conditions as a result of the increasing exposure of domestic and foreign economies to competitive forces.
The progressive reduction of trade barriers will expose industry
to increasing competition in both the home market and world
markets. The response of employee organisations and industry
to this development is an issue of critical importance to collective
bargaining, to the nature and structure of the economy, and to
economic policy generally.

Heretofore, the response of employee organisations and industries effected by trade liberalisation measures has been the sort of
response one has become accustomed to expect from groups
pursuing their short-term self-interest: they have sought protection against foreign competition in the domestic market, and
assistance against international competition in foreign markets –
quotas, tariffs, subsidies and domestic content barriers to foreign
competition in the home market, and subsidies, low interest
credit terms, and government promotion and development of
foreign markets. Seldom is reference made to the question of who
will bear the costs of such barriers, which invariably become
manifested in the price structure.

In a world that has agreed to lower all barriers to trade,
protective measures will be tolerated in periods of crisis only.
Over the long run, the most effective measures against foreign
competition in the home market and in foreign markets are the
quality of goods and services offered on the market and their
supply prices. A retrospective examination of the structural
changes in the economy over time and the factors responsible for
them will establish that the competitive forces of the international economy are significantly stronger than the forces mar-
shalled by governments, employee organisations and giant
corporate establishments. Even tightly controlled centrally
planned economies have to buck their continuous pressures.

This issue will gain increasing importance in the near future,
as developing countries demand unimpeded and assisted access
into the markets of developed countries, and as computer and
telecommunications technology reduces communication barriers. Management will find itself under increasing pressure to
develop new products and processes, to re-organise and restructure in an effort to remain competitive; and unions will find
themselves increasingly involved in the responses of industry to
the challenges of international competition. The luxury enjoyed
by them heretofore in formulating their demands on the basis of

established patterns and placing the onus on management to accommodate them, will become a matter of the historical record.

WINNERS, AND LOSERS

The victorious are not always the winners in management–labour conflicts; the costs of victory may exceed by far the costs of defeat. It is often problematical whether the victor or the defeated adversary is the net gainer. A union leader can claim victory in extracting another dollar per hour, but that additional dollar per hour may come from members of the union, not from the employer. If robots can perform some of the functions of workers, and if more efficient instruments can increase the productivity of workers, then victory for the union will be defeat for some of the members of the union. The funds required for the dollar increase will be obtained from the workers that will be replaced by capital equipment. If payroll is $20 m and there are 1000 workers, the replacement of 100 workers will provide the enterprise $2 m, which will enable it to grant the remaining 900 workers an increase of up to 11.1 per cent.

The positive aspects of this outcome are twofold: one is that it forces management to seek out instruments and processes that will increase productivity, i.e. to produce the same or a larger output with a smaller labour force; and the other is that the workers who retain their jobs will enjoy an increase in incomes. The negative aspects are found in the workers who will lose their jobs, and in buyers of the goods and services who may have to pay higher prices. In the long-run, after all adjustments to products and processes are completed, the vanquished may turn out to be the actual victors, and the victors may turn out to be the vanquished.

This is the historical reality. Most union victories over enterprises which could not accommodate demanded increases in pay with their existing processes, have been at the cost of employment. In some such instances, as in the coal industry, for example, the actions were conscious and deliberate: it was recognised that unless the industry were forced to restructure, modernise and consolidate, low wages and deplorable working conditions would continue to prevail. The increases in wages, regardless of the ability of individual companies to pay, forced modernisations and consolidations, the outcome of which was abandonment of sub-marginal mines, takeovers, consolidations, increases in productivity, substantial increases in pay, significant improvements in conditions of work, notable improvements in non-wage terms of employment, and very substantial unemployment of miners. Whereas in other industries, such as the automobile industry, the actions manifested a reckless disregard of market place realities. Both labour and management failed to observe the signals of technological imperatives in the accommodation of each other's short-term self-interests. They failed to note that the patterns they followed each year or every few years in wage and price accommodations constituted an open invitation to potential international competitors who exercised more effective market responsive controls over wages and prices. It was inevitable that new technological instruments and processes would be put into effect which would challenge the quality, efficiency and price of existing products. The victories that labour and management had over one another, and the victories that both of them had over the North American consumer, were eventually paid by the thousands of workers who became disemployed from the automobile industry and industries related to it operationally, and by significantly reduced profits. The disregard of market realities by management and labour caused in effect the transfer of employment in automobile manufacturing and related industries from North America to Japan.

The experience with the automobile industry contains evident lessons on what can be expected if management and labour disregard international economic realities and pursue established policies and mutually accommodative practices designed to serve their short-term self-interest.

THE ISSUES OF WAGE AND PRICE REGULATION

The issue of wage and price regulation has become the subject of intense discussion between governments, business and labour in recent years, and will bear significantly on relations between labour and management in future.[15]

Serious conflicts should be anticipated, since regulation infringes on the freedom of enterprises to set prices, and on the freedom of labour and management to negotiate on wages. Yet, it must be recognised that when markets become increasingly ineffective in their price-making and allocative functions, alternative mechanisms must be found to ensure that the making of prices by interest groups are not negative to the economy and society at large. When markets set wages freely, and demand and supply of occupations respond to the set wages without direct or indirect intervention from anyone, there would be no reason to regulate. But, when someone intervenes on the demand side or on the supply side, by restricting the numbers entering different occupations, or by regulating the functions that different occupations can perform, the wage can no longer be regarded as market determined, and the allocation of people amongst occupations and employments can no longer be viewed as efficient.[16]

Application of the standard criteria used in the categorisation of markets as perfect and imperfect, to the labour market, to product markets and to the organisation of industry, would lead to the conclusion that they are highly imperfect. Imperfect markets cause distortions in the wage and price structure, which, in turn, cause misallocations in human and material resources. In such case, some form of regulation of wages and prices is deemed desirable and necessary for improvements in efficiency in the allocation and utilisation of human and material resources, and for greater equity in the distribution of the ends of the economy.

Assuming the indicated cause and effect relationship to be substantially correct, that is, that market imperfections are responsible for distortions in wages and prices, and the misallocation of resources and inefficiencies, the question then would be whether to remove the imperfections or to regulate the outcomes of the imperfections. Which is the more possible, and which is potentially the more effective? To assist in the development of competition in a non-competitive market or to regulate the prices of enterprises which are not regulated by market forces? To break-up monopolies or regulate their charges? Discussions about the desirability and necessity of regulation constitute an implicit admission that it is perhaps easier to regulate the outcomes of imperfections, than to remove the imperfections. It is an admission that the organisations and institutions which influence and control demand and supply, and prevent markets from clearing, have gained permanence in the economic system. If it is not possible to remove monopolies and collusive arrangements amongst enterprises and between enterprises and organisations, and if it is not possible to regulate effectively their activities so that the outcomes of their decisions will approximate the outcomes of competitive markets, then regulation of the outcomes would be the next best alternative. Which suggests that if enterprises and organisations wish to avoid the introduction of wage and price regulations, they would have to demonstrate that the prevailing wages and prices are at levels that would be expected to prevail under perfectly competitive market conditions.

In a democratic society, effective regulation is conditional upon recognition of its desirability by both the public at large and those affected by the regulation. No regulation can be effective if those affected by it believe to be aggrieved by it, or believe it to be discriminatory and inequitable. Organised labour can be expected to oppose the regulation of wages, or given their regulation, to render the regulatory process ineffective, if it believed that prices and profits were not likely to be, or were not, regulated as vigorously and effectively; if it believed that the existing distribution of the ends of the economy was inequitable and regulation was likely to perpetuate the inequitable distribution; or if it expected that the ultimate outcome of the regulatory process was likely to be negative to non-management employees. The lessons of history, and the experiences in countries which have had varying forms of wage and price regulations would provide labour the grounds for concern: the tendency has been to subordinate the private interests of employees to the general interest.[17]

Nevertheless, in recent years movements in wages and prices in most industrial countries have tended to diverge rather significantly from what would normally have been expected from the prevailing labour market conditions and product market conditions: wages increased when unemployment was rising, and prices were rising when demand was falling. Although explanations for these unusual happenings have varied in their detail, there has been general consensus on one causal factor, namely, the existence of organisational and institutional imperfections in both markets – governmental interventions, activities of regulatory bodies, employee organisations, marketing boards, oligopolies in manufacturing, distribution and finance, and such other. Market forces have either not been allowed to manifest themselves fully in the determination of wages and prices, or they have been manipulated to provide support to wages and prices established by the administrative process. In other words, surpluses were either not allowed to manifest themselves in the market place and influence the administratively set prices, or they were removed from the market place to create scarcity and thereby provide market support to the administratively set prices.

Departures of wages and prices from market realities in periods of inflation and unemployment invite focus on the role of non-market sources responsible for their behaviour, and generate public pressures for government intervention and regulation. Labour and management have always reacted negatively to the possibility of wage and price regulation, the first alleging that regulation will interfere with the collective bargaining process, as if the process produces the most appropriate wages for the economy at any given time, and the second alleging that regulation will interfere with the market process, as if prices were determined by the free operation of market forces. Their unwillingness to subordinate their private interests to the general interest in periods of economic crises, invites government intervention and regulation.

Regulation has had its supporters and its detractors:[18] its supporters hold to the view that regulation is more effective and less costly to the economy than the alternative measures; whereas its detractors insist that regulation distorts the allocation of resources and bears down on equity and efficiency. The detractors case is problematical: it is based on the false premise that resources are allocated by free market forces, and that the market allocates the ends of the economic process efficiently and equitably. The costs to the economy and society of the muddling about policies in the period 1978–82 have been enormous. It is doubtful that regulation of wages and prices would have involved the enormous costs in unemployment, in distorted allocation of resources, and in reduced productivity that monetary and other measures have inflicted on the economy and society at large.[19]

EQUITY IN WAGE REGULATION

One of the fundamental principles in wage and price regulations should be that the *relative* living standards of individuals, families and groups of individuals will not be altered significantly during the period when regulations are in force: that is, the effect of the regulations on individual real incomes after tax, whatever the source of incomes, will be the same on all. This principle has been violated in every country that experimented with wage and price regulations. Somehow recipients of profits, rents, fees, commissions and interest, and persons in high level managerial and administrative positions, seem to find it possible to escape the full impact of regulations, and sellers of goods and services seem to find it possible to raise their prices. It would appear, distributive justice is always the first to suffer when regulations are put into effect. Why should it not be the opposite? Since low income recipients have limited opportunities for downward substitution in consumption of goods and services, it would be more just economically to guarantee their subsistence at a cost to high income recipients.

Advocates of wage and price regulations have been criticised for allegedly minimising the implications for income distribution and the allocation of resources. In theory distortions can be avoided and indeed some existing distortions can be corrected through an effective system of regulations. But, the evidence from countries which have experienced the results of regulations, suggest that in practice significant distortions take place:[20] firstly, the regulation of wages tends to induce the introduction of non-wage incentives, which cause "wage drift" and influence regional, industrial and occupational mobility of labour at the expense of firms that are not able to introduce such incentives; secondly, since effective enforcement in the private sector is influenced by evidence of their enforcement in the public sector, there has been a tendency on the part of governments to insist upon the rigid application of the rules on the wages and salaries of all employees who are paid out of public revenues. When changes in wages and salaries in the private sector are in line with the regulations all is well; but, when, as frequently happens, they are out of line, holding down the wages and salaries of employees who are paid out of public revenue means that such

employees are being used as instruments for the effective enforcement of an unenforceable public policy. This is discriminatory,
with the attendant results of income redistribution in favour of
the private sector, and given demand for labour in the private
sector, manpower relocation in favour of the private sector.
Some would applaud such results, not realising perhaps that an
economic system in which governments play an active role as
participants and regulators requires an efficient public service. If
the well qualified and efficient are drawn into the private sector,
not only the public sector but the private sector as well will
suffer. Thirdly, for the same reasons as those advanced above,
social security incomes are held down, resulting in a negative
redistribution of income. Again, some would applaud such a
result, motivated largely by the notion that most social security
income recipients are parasites. To the extent that they are
parasites, regulations other than wage and price controls should
prevent them from feeding on the efforts of others. But, to the
extent that they are pensioners, children, handicapped and those
unable to work for various reasons, it is unjust to hold down their
standard of living in order to ensure the effectiveness of wage and
price stabilisation.

It can be argued, of course, that the distortions associated
with wage and price regulations are not as widespread nor as
substantial as are the distortions of substantial wage and price
increases. Those favouring regulations point to the fact that
historically wages and salaries in the public sector have tended
to lag behind the increase in prices and increases in wages and
salaries in the private sector; and that social security incomes
have always tended to lag behind both prices and wages and
salaries generally. The two groups are likely to fair better within
a system of regulations, because the onus will be on governments
to show that they are not being used deliberately as instruments
of control to ensure a reasonable degree of effectiveness in the
application of wage and price regulations.

Nevertheless, it is regrettable that neither workers nor the
public generally have been informed on the implications of wage
and price regulations. The public cannot be a rational participant in the debate and cannot be expected to declare itself on the
issue without such information.

Organised labour has traditionally opposed wage controls.
This does not mean that labour leaders do not understand or

appreciate the problem of rising wages in periods of excessive unemployment and/or inflation; it is rather a manifestation of concern that wage controls, whether statutory or voluntary, will result in income gains by other groups in society at the expense of labour. Discussions with labour leaders on the issue have led to the conclusion that expression of opposition should be interpreted broadly to mean "labour will not lead the parade to moderation". This is based on the bitter experiences of some older leaders who led the parade to moderation in the national interest at the beginning of the Second World War, only to discover that industry did not follow, and whereas workers were suffering eroded incomes, industry profits were rising. Barbara Wooton contrasts the problem of voluntary income restraint with the problem of voluntary disarmanent:

> Every nation would be only too willing to disarm if every other nation was certain to do the same: but nobody dares to be the first, lest another should break the rules.[21]

Therefore, whether voluntary or statutory, the rate of increase in wages can only be regulated in conjunction with the rate of increase in other incomes. The case for voluntarism is that reason must be given if people are to observe the regulations; and the most compelling reason that one can provide is the observance of agreed upon regulations by non-wage income recipients.

In the absence of agreement for voluntary restraint in wage demands and in the setting of salaries, fees, commissions and other forms of payment for manpower services, and in the absence of restraint in the setting of prices for goods and services, the only effective alternative to their regulation would be the confiscation of increases in excess of a range of approved norms. In relation to wages and salaries, the norms may vary in accordance with their levels, to ensure that the lowest income groups are assured their subsistence; and in relation to prices, they may vary in accordance with the level of profits.

The nature of discriminatory application of such confiscatory measures will depend upon the objectives that are being sought. For example, discrimination with a bias favouring the low-paid will redistribute incomes downward. Is such incidental levelling of incomes a predetermined goal of controls? On the other hand, increases in wages and profits in excess of the established norms may be exempt in employments which have been having difficulties in attracting adequate supplies of labour, and industries which undertake to invest the excess profits. Both of these are discriminatory relative to industries and employments that are not given the same advantages, and it must be shown that such discrimination is justified on grounds of economic efficiency.[22]

6 Bargaining in the Public Sector

INTRODUCTION

Two related developments have had a most profound effect on labour and labour-management relations in the past thirty years: one is the very significant decrease in the proportion of the labour force that is engaged in the production of goods and the provisions of traditional services, such as transportation; and the other is the rapid increase of employment in the public service and enterprises funded largely by the public treasuries. The first is manifested in increasing proportions of the labour force entering into employments that have been difficult to organise, such as professional and technical, clerical, consultative, and general services. The second is manifested in the organisation of public service employees, and employees of enterprises and agencies funded by public monies, such as teachers and hospital employees.

There is a triple significance in these changes: one is that the power of the traditional, largely goods-based, trade unions has been diminishing, and with that the stability in the labour-management scene has been significantly eroded. Notwithstanding the impression of toughness in "blue-collar" unionism, the traditional unions of tradesmen, construction workers, automobile workers, steelworkers, transportation workers, textile workers, have been generally stable, conservative and responsible. Stability and long-standing experience remove from the process two elements of conflict: the feeling of insecurity and a sense of uncertainty.

The second change is related to this issue: the increasing dominance of public service unions in the labour scene is increasingly eroding the relative stability that has existed in labour-management relations, replacing it with insecurity and uncertainty. An entirely different environment has emerged, one which the traditional unions do not quite understand: the guide-posts of costs, prices and profits do not exist; there are no competitors; and there are no capitalists bent on the exploitation of workers. The opposite side are representatives of the public, which is themselves.

The third change is the impetus that the organisation of "white-collar" public service employees is giving to the organ-isation of "white-collar" workers in the private sector.[1] The organisation, bargaining and striking by professional and techni-cal personnel in the public sector, many of them with managerial responsibilities, and the organisation, bargaining and striking by professors, teachers, secretaries, clerks and typists, nurses, po-licemen and firemen, and even doctors, has given the process of collective bargaining a considerable degree of social legitimacy. It is inevitable that the counterpart occupations in the private sector will be influenced, particularly when the bargaining out-comes indicate gains in terms of employment and conditions of work relative to the private sector.

Almost fifteen years ago, a widely recognised authority on labour and labour–management relations wrote:

> The advent of employee organisations and collective bargain-ing to the public sector is the most significant development in the industrial relations field of the last 30 years. In addition to the more obvious implications for employees, public officials and the art of government, it may have important effects on the labor movement and on labor-management relations in the private sector.[2]

The nature of collective bargaining that will evolve with the shift in employee organisation and power from the largely goods-based "blue-collar" segment of the labour force to the services-producing "white-collar" segment, and particularly to public service employments, will depend on the response of society at large and that of organised groups within society, to the bargaining processes and measures that have been adopted from the goods-producing private sector. Are the bargaining processes (including the strike) of the goods-producing private sector appropriate for the services-producing private sector? Are they appropriate for the public sector and institutions funded by public treasuries? The relative hardships resulting from the interruption in production notwithstanding, people perceive differently the interruption of schooling services, health services, garbage collection services, or postal services, from interruptions in the production of steel, automobiles or lumber. The services are largely rendered to the people directly and effect the people directly;[3] whereas the interruptions in goods production may not effect them at all. It is immaterial to argue that the perception is based largely on habit and convenience; in most instances the real harm to the public is no greater from the interruption of services to which the public is accustomed, than the harm emanating from the interruption in the production of widgets. Nevertheless, should public opinion become established firmly that interruptions in certain services will not be tolerated, then bargaining procedures and processes will have to be changed in ways which will make bargaining effective without resort to strike action. In other words, negotiating procedures will have to change to make "no strike bargaining" effective.

THE ORGANISATION OF PUBLIC SERVICE EMPLOYEES FOR BARGAINING

A long standing advocate of public service bargaining, Myron Lieberman, has recently re-examined the rationale and implications of the process, and concluded that collective bargaining in the public service of the United States was not a desirable public policy and was not necessary from the standpoint of equity considerations.[4] His conclusion is based on the following arguments:

1. Contrary to allegations that public service employees are behind private sector employees and that collective bargaining is a necessary process to bring about catch-up gains, public service employees have two advantages that are not available to private sector employees, namely, job security and statutory benefits. The first is bestowed on them by tradition; they do not need bargaining to secure it for them. Whereas the second involves a wide range of benefits that are provided to them by statute or by administrative regulation – retirement benefits, separation benefits, disability benefits, sick leave, maternity leave, etc.; issues over which

private sector employees have long struggled and many still do not have.

2. Bargaining in the public sector is largely a political contest, not an economic one. The parties engage in posturing and exaggeration to influence public opinion. Furthermore, conflicts become institutionalised, with harmful effects on the rendering of public services.

3. The overall impact of bargaining on public sector productivity is likely to be negative. Job security and the absence of market restraints on the demands of public service employees tend to have negative effects on efforts to improve efficiency.

These arguments have caused Lieberman to conclude that collective bargaining in the public sector is in conflict with cost effectiveness in the rendering of public services, it has negative effects on the quality of public services, and conflicts with citizen participation in the control of public services.

Collective bargaining need not, of course, become the cause of such undesirable outcomes. After all, collective bargaining is nothing more than a change in the process of determining terms and conditions of employment, from unilateral managerial to collective, involving the participation of employee representatives. Negative outcomes are most often the result of inadequate and imperfect criteria, and the result of weaknesses in comparative information used in the determination of terms and conditions, not the result of the process itself.[5] On the contrary, collective bargaining often provides an opportunity for trade-offs that may not be feasible when terms and conditions of employment are set unilaterally. For example, it is quite conceivable to seek some sort of trade-off between employment security and wages. It should not be difficult to put a wage cost to each per cent of unemployment and to trade that off against the rates of pay in employments that enjoy relatively low rates of unemployment. The introduction of such a pay policy unilaterally by management will most likely cause conflict. Collective bargaining provides an opportunity for discussion, which even in the absence of trade-offs has educative value. It brings to attention employment realities and preferences, which can be translated into costs and become reflected in the wage and salary structure.

In relation to the private sector, four claims are made in favour of collective bargaining: it contributes to industrial peace;

the participation of workers in their own governance contributes to industrial democracy; the collectivity of organised workers contributes to the democratic political process through worker representation; and collective representation redresses the problem of unequal bargaining between employers and individual workers.[6] All of these claims apply equally to the public sector.

It is problematical whether the interests of society at large are being served when public service employees are prohibited from participation in the determination of their terms and conditions of employment. Considering that all other employees have a legal right to engage in such activity there must exist compelling reasons to deny that right to public servants. The compelling reasons commonly used by governments relate to the essentiality of public services, and to the commitments that governments make to the public at large to provide public services, neither of which has any validity in a general sense. Some public services are deemed essential and perhaps are essential, and their continuing provision must be ensured; but all public services cannot be so categorised. As to the commitment by governments to provide them, if governments were held fully responsible for the promises they make, few of them will be able to defend their continuing existence for longer than perhaps one week.

There is no justification in denying public servants the right to engage in collective determination of the terms and conditions of their employment. There is justification in denying public servants (and non-public servants) the right to discontinue and enforce the discontinuance of social services deemed necessary for the maintenance of health and safety, which suggests the need for alternative dispute settlement arrangements in such cases, which will produce just and equitable collective agreements.

Advocacy of collective bargaining in the public sector need not mean, of course, that all terms and conditions of employment in the public sector must be determined through the collective bargaining process. Sandra Christensen argues[7] that the pay scales of public sector employees should be set by an independent agency on the basis of private sector comparability. Since market criteria cannot be used in public sector pay determination, the application of private sector comparability would mean that the market conditions that become reflected in private sector pay settlements will also become reflected in public sector pay settlements.

In reality, the critical issue is not whether public service employees should have the same rights as other employees; the critical issue is rather whether the principles and practices of industrial unionism are appropriate for public sector employments. The absence of a market price for the services produced by public service employees makes it difficult to establish market criteria for the determination of their wages and salaries. Yet, it is critical that the criteria used in the public sector reflect the realities of production and employment in the market sector.

A word of caution is warranted: alternative arrangements can only work successfully when the outcomes approximate the outcomes of the collective bargaining process in the short run, and the outcomes of the market in the long run. Departures of outcomes for whatever reason, and particularly departures which manifest the use of public servants as instruments for the execution of questionable economic policies will violate the principles of equity and efficiency, and will thereby maintain a state of conflict in the short-run and disequilibrium in the long run. In other words, the denial to some public service employees of the right to strike, and the determination of their pay by some tribunal will stand effective only as long as the effected public servants are provided with terms and conditions of employment that are deemed fair and equitable relative to the terms and conditions established through the bargaining process. Employees are not likely to agitate and strike over the right to strike, all other things being equal. But, they will strike, and will defy government orders to work, if they are placed at a comparative disadvantage relative to their counterparts in the private sector or relative to their counterparts in other political jurisdictions. Equity does not mean equality; but, when terms and conditions are unequal, equity considerations dictate that the unequal conditions be justified on the basis of rational economic criteria. For example, if the wages of public servants were to be set below the wages of their counterparts in the private sector, or if the wages of public servants in a given political jurisdiction were to be set below the wages of their counterparts in another political jurisdiction within the national economy, equity considerations would dictate that the inequalities be justified on the basis of generally acceptable economic criteria. The avoidance of conflict in an environment of discriminatory restrictions on freedom to participate collectively in the determination of terms and conditions of employment, and where the outcomes of the alternative processes are unequal, is conditional on the existence of a sense of equitable treatment *on balance* – that the inequality in some terms and conditions of employment is offset by reverse inequality in some other terms and conditions of employment.

BARGAINING ISSUES IN THE PUBLIC SECTOR

There is no superior alternative to collective bargaining for the settlement of terms and conditions of employment. The possible alternatives, amongst which there are the unilateral decisions of employers still in effect where collective bargaining does not exist, compulsory arbitration, government decrees, all suffer greater weaknesses than the process of collective determination.

It is critical, however, that there be a clear understanding what the purpose of collective bargaining is, what collective bargaining can do, and what it cannot do.[8] The collective bargaining process is, and will remain, an effective mechanism only as long as it is used for the settlement of terms and conditions of employment for which it is designed. Since the outcome of the process is agreement between the two parties, it cannot be an effective process for issues on which agreement is not possible, such as, for example, the distribution of income in the nation, the merits of capitalism versus socialism, the introduction of "industrial democracy" in the enterprise, whatever that may mean, and such other.

Another relevant issue concerns the appropriateness for the public sector of collective bargaining procedures and processes (including the strike) developed largely in the context of private sector conditions and environments. The issue is not whether public sector employees should have the right to organise, whether they should be represented by organisations and individuals of their choice in bargaining, or whether their terms of employment and conditions of work should be set down in writing. The issue is rather whether the processes and procedures used in the private sector in arriving at the terms of employment and conditions of work are appropriate for the public sector.[9]

In the government sector, the reaction of the public at large must be taken into account, which both governments and their organised employees make every effort to influence.[10] The public is the third party in the bargaining process, invisible but highly influential. It is not uncommon to find ultimate outcomes of bargaining processes that reflect more the reaction of the public to the positions taken by the two parties, than the merits of the respective positions.

In the non-government public sector, the government is the second non-participating, yet highly influential party in the bargaining process. Since the ultimate outcome often depends on it, the parties to the bargaining process expend as much effort in attempts to influence the public at large and cause the government to take a position and commit itself, as they do in negotiation with one another. Indeed, often they do not even make an effort to negotiate. The game that is being played is similar to that played by the railways and their employees for many decades: the railways would say "the demands of the unions are justified, but we cannot do much until the government gives a commitment that it will allow an increase in our charges to offset the additional costs". There followed then pressures by both the railways and the unions on the government to allow increases in charges or failing that to grant the railways compensatory subsidies, and counter-pressures by shippers not to permit increases in charges. Essentially the same game is being played by school boards and their teachers, by hospitals and their staffs, and by others whose budgets are determined by governments and the taxpayers.

In view of this, is the bargaining process in the public sector organised appropriately for effective bargaining and just and equitable outcomes? If governments and the public have so much critical influence on the outcomes, they should be informed fully and accurately on the bargaining issues, and the positions taken on them by the two parties. This cannot be achieved with the information disseminated by the parties through the media. Government and the public should have direct access to the bargaining process. It is necessary perhaps that governments and the public be represented in an observer capacity during negotiations. The often used argument that elected governments and boards, and government appointed boards represent the public, is not a valid argument. Governments and boards have vested interests which often depart from the interests of the public at large; furthermore, it is not uncommon for governments and boards to become captives of their bureaucracies. Objectivity in examination of the issues and positions taken by the respective parties dictates neutrality. Governments and boards, whether they be elected or appointed boards, cannot be neutral in their approach to bargaining with the organisations of employees.

This issue relates also to the composition of the dispute–settlement machinery for the public sector. In the private sector the government steps in as a neutral party offering or imposing mediation services. Can it do the same in the public sector, where it is involved, directly or indirectly as one of the parties? It cannot and it should not! It can appoint an independent authority *acceptable to both parties* to investigate and inform the public on the dispute, but it cannot itself become involved. It is indefensible and unethical for a party in a dispute to become also the party that would dictate the terms and conditions of settlement.

A critical condition for effective collective bargaining and dispute settlement in the public sector is the neutrality of government. Involvement of the government, directly or indirectly, actually or potentially, erodes the bargaining process of its logic and rationale. No bargainer will bargain on the merits of the case if there exists a possibility of government involvement and the imposition of terms and conditions of employment motivated by political considerations. Instead of bargaining, efforts will then be directed to influencing government decisions.

THE STRIKE AS AN INSTRUMENT OF COLLECTIVE BARGAINING IN THE PUBLIC SECTOR

When the appropriateness of private-sector collective bargaining for the public sector is questioned, most critical comments are directed towards the strike. In the private sector, the strike is recognised as part of the bargaining process itself – a phase of the process put into effect when all other approaches fail to yield the expected target outcomes. Is the strike an appropriate measure for the public sector?[11]

From the standpoint of individual employees there should be no basic difference between private sector employment and public sector employment: the individual employee sells services, and in pursuit of self-interest will sell services to whoever offers the best terms of employment and conditions of work, on balance. Equally, in pursuit of self-interest the individual employee will withdraw the services from any employer who does not offer terms of employment and conditions of work which the employee deems equitable and desirable. The implicit general freedom to choose amongst alternatives and sell services to those who offer the most favourable terms on balance, and withdraw the sale of services from those who offer terms that are not so favourable on balance, is fundamental to the private enterprise democratic process. In this context, the individual employee has a legitimate right to oppose any measure that would prohibit or restrain the exercise of that freedom. Measures which prohibit some employees from certain actions, which other employees exercise freely, are discriminatory measures. Discriminatory measures must be justified on grounds that are superior to the grounds they violate. It is natural that the average employee will oppose measures that will restrain the freedom of choice in the pursuit of self-interest, when the purpose of the restraint is to enhance or preserve someone else's freedom of choice in the pursuit of self-interest.

Most calls for the prohibition of strikes are motivated by self-interest: parents who find it inconvenient to have their children at home; businessmen who have to change their travel plans when the planes do not fly; the inconvenience and cost of having to find alternative means for the conveyance of information because of a postal strike; the inconvenience of having to find alternative means of conveyance because of a transit strike. Inconvenience cannot be recognised as a legitimate basis for the imposition of restraints on employees in the pursuit of their self-interest.

More than inconvenience to some, and impairment in the pursuit of self-interest to others, must be involved to justify legal restraints on the freedom of employees to withdraw their services temporarily, regardless whether the employees are in public service employment or private service employment. Arguments to the effect that strikes in the public sector are incompatible with the implicit undertaking of the public authority to provide services without interruption, are founded on a special interpretation of the public authority's commitment. The public authority is committed to provide an efficient and reliable postal service. It does not necessarily mean that the service must be provided without interruption or it must be provided two or three times per day, seven days per week. It was a time when the service was provided three times per day, six days per week. The frequency has changed over time and it now stands at one time per day, five days per week in many places, and no service on a number of statutory holidays. The inconvenience of such changes, to which the public has become accustomed, is not much different from the inconvenience of interruptions caused by temporary withdrawals of services. Similarly, the commitment of the public authority to provide educational services does not mean those services must be provided without interruption. Indeed, interruptions are sanctioned for teachers' conventions, family vacations, holidays, football and basketball tournaments, the summer break, and all sorts of other reasons. What is the difference between such interruptions and interruptions caused by the temporary withdrawal of services by teachers? The difference is that interruptions caused by the withdrawal of services are not scheduled in advance and thereby interfere with established patterns of family life. They are an inconvenience; they do not constitute any danger to the health, safety or even to the welfare of the community. When interruptions are scheduled in advance, appropriate accommodative adjustments are made, and the interruptions pass without notice.

The argument for prohibition becomes even weaker when extended to public services generally: it is difficult to find many government services whose interruption is likely to cause serious damage to the welfare of the community at large: legislatures have long recesses; the judiciary takes holidays; Cabinets have long interruptions in meetings; and there are hundreds of occupations and employments in the public service whose counterparts in the private sector take strike action with no negative effects on the community. What terrible act will befall on the community at large if government lawyers, economists, statisticians, and sociologists, planners, advisors, and secretaries, employees of liquor stores, recreational facilities, cafeterias, and auto licensing bureaus were to go on strike? Clearly, it is not the essentiality of services that motivates governments in prohibiting or restraining strikes by public service employees; it is political self-interest.

The issues are somewhat different in relation to services which involve the health and safety of the community: it is not possible to schedule in advance the on-set of illness, accidents, fires and other developments that threaten health, life and property, and it is difficult to provide even a critical minimum of service outside the established system, whether that system be police services, fire services or hospital services. It is true that individual communities have had interruptions in such services without apparent negative effects, but in most such instances the interruptions were of short duration, and adequate emergency services were provided by the organisations of striking employees, and by adjoining communities.

The fact that individual communities have had interruptions in *essential* services and came out of them without widespread and unmanageable threats to life, health and safety suggests that even essentiality is not an adequate ground for the *total* prohibition of interruptions. The critical issue appears to be the duration of the interruption, the provision of a critical minimum of emergency service within the system by members of the striking organisation, and the constituency that is effected by the interruption. In other words, experience suggests that the critical issue is not the interruption of essential services, but the *length* of interruption; which means in turn that an alternative to prohibition of interruptions in the rendering of full complements of essential services would be some procedures which would limit their duration. The only qualification to this relates to the availability of emergency services: any length, however short, is conditional on the availability of *a critical minimum* of emergency service. The public authority has an obligation to protect the community against acts of violence, and to ensure reasonable protection against threats to health, life and property. Unless those rendering the essential service provide the critical minimum of service that is required, the public authority has a social duty to prohibit the interruption, and impose alternative processes for the settlement of disputes. It is recognised that the provision of any amount of service reduces somewhat the effectiveness of a strike. Nevertheless, the organisation of employees providing essential services must consider the disadvantage of reduced effectiveness against the disadvantage of prohibition, which is the possible alternative.[12]

In relation to the constituency that is effected by an interruption, the greater the constituency the more critical the problem, since it precludes the possibility of using the services of adjoining constituencies for emergencies.

The public has been generally negative towards interruptions in services it regards essential, which includes virtually all services whose interruption would tend to inconvenience it, and has demanded the imposition of compulsory arbitration as an alternative. But, this is a generalisation. An examination of public attitudes will reveal an interesting paradox. There is greater tolerance of interruptions in services involving the so-called "blue-collar" workers, than those involving "white-collar" workers. For example, interruptions in educational services caused by caretakers appear to be accepted more readily than interruptions caused by teachers. Similarly, greater tolerance appears to be expressed towards interruptions of hospital services by maintenance workers or kitchen workers, than by nurses. It is perhaps a manifestation of the predominant social values, and a perception of proper behaviour by different occupational groups. Teachers are expected to demonstrate a higher level of social responsibility than school caretakers. Why this should be so is not clear. Nevertheless, it suggests that society's response to interruptions in social services tends to differ in accordance with expected appropriate social behaviour of individual occupational groups, notwithstanding the increasing frequency of picket lines by teachers, nurses, engineers, doctors, and scores of other "white-collar" and white-coated workers.

The social values that governed employment in many public sector activities in the past have changed radically: public servants, such as nurses and teachers, have stopped accepting psychic income for the highly valued work functions they perform, and demand instead real payments and improvements in their conditions of work. Their cause has been just: if society puts a high social value to their services, and regards their services indispensable to the social process, then society must demonstrate its willingness to provide them with incomes and social advantages that are commensurate with that social value. It is significant to note that even after the notable improvements in the relative wages of public sector employees in recent years, many occupations continue to be lower on the occupational wage scale than they are on the occupational social scale. Which means that the social ranking of some occupations, nurses and teachers amongst them, continues to be higher than their ranking on the salary scale.[13] If the social ranking reflects the value that society puts to the services that are rendered by these occupations, then the question arises whether that value should not be reflected in their salaries.

Social value is, of course, only one of the variables that enters into the determination of wages and salaries, and it is the variable most likely responsible for the differences between social ranking and wage ranking: the relatively high social ranking of an occupation tends to induce more people to enter into it than demand for it at prevailing wages, which would depress the wage, while relatively low social ranking may cause fewer people to enter the occupation than the demand for it, which would cause the wage to increase. Implicit in this is the proposition that the social ranking of occupations contains an element of cost which people bear or claim, depending on the occupations they choose to enter. Those who choose occupations that have relatively high social ranking would be expected to be willing to bear the cost of their preference in the form of lower pay than the alternative occupations available to them which carry lower social ranking, whereas those who enter occupations with relatively low social ranking could be expected to claim the cost of entering and performing work activities that society regards negatively. It was common in the past to regard most social service occupations as of the first category, and all manual occupations as of the second. In more recent times attitudes have changed: public service employees, particularly those engaged in activities to which society attributes relatively high values, seem to believe that society has an obligation to ensure that the terms and conditions of their employment reflect the social value of their activities.

Related to this is the issue of what public service employees refer to as "double standard" – restrictions on their freedom to pursue their self-interest in ways other employees are legally able to do. Their argument has been that if society should deem it necessary, for whatever reasons, to restrict their freedom as employees to pursue their self-interest in ways other employees are permitted to do, such as strike activity, for example, then society must provide them with alternative compensatory benefits, such as guaranteed employment, higher incomes, superior retirement arrangements, longer holidays, and such other.

The responses of governments to expectations of public service employees have varied widely, depending on political philosophies, nature of services rendered, pressures by interest groups, tradition, and nature of experience with arbitration processes. Some governments have sought to educate the public on the difference between essentiality and inconvenience, and limited the invocation of compulsory processes to very essential services only, such as hospital, police and fire; some prohibit the interruption of any public services, and have instituted arbitration processes as a permanent element to the collective bargaining process; whereas other, have not prohibited the interruption of any services, but have not allowed many to take place, and where some have been allowed, they have not been allowed to last long.[14] Experience has taught most, although *not* all, governments that prohibition of strikes does not deter strikes in democratic political systems. If prohibitions are to be effective in preventing strike activity, they must be accompanied with alternative systems of conflict resolution that are acceptable to both parties.[15]

The responses of employee organisations to restrains on strike activity have varied, too: some, such as policemen and firemen have in many instances elected arbitration as the ultimate process; whereas other, such as teachers, have generally rejected arbitration. Generally, attitudes of organisations have been influenced by their experience with the arbitration process, and by their anticipation of arbitration outcomes, founded largely on their reading of public attitudes towards them and their cause.[16]

It is often said that alternative systems to dispute settlement would not be necessary if there were no disputes. Therefore, the focus should be in the direction of eliminating the causes of disputes, not in the direction of seeking alternative methods to deal with the disputes. Although this is a logical argument, it is not realistic: as long as there are managers and managed, decision-makers and implementors of decisions, and, indeed, as long as there are different opinions on how things are to be done, disputes will take place and there will be a need for some form of dispute settlement mechanism. From the standpoint of the ultimate outcome of a bargaining process, including strikes, mediation, conciliation and arbitration, it is not certain whether collective bargaining is not a preferred process to one where disputes are resolved by majority decisions, where a very substantial minority may remain dissatisfied with the outcome.[17]

Another critical problem in public sector collective bargaining is the role of government as employer and legislator: the government negotiates, and if it does not like the outcome of the bargaining process (strike, slowdown, work-to-rule) legislates adjustments to the collective bargaining process, (by ordering employees to perform their work without interruptions and disruptions), institutes alternative processes (fact finding commission, arbitration, conciliation) or imposes new terms of employment and conditions of work. This is hardly the sort of balance in institutional powers that can foster the evolution of effective collective bargaining. Even if the invocation of legislative powers were limited to instances of serious threat to social order and community welfare, the legislative area of government should be separated from the employer area. Such separation can be achieved if negotiations on behalf of the government were conducted by a quasi judicial government agency, with powers to impose on government the terms and conditions negotiated on its behalf.

The shift in employment from goods production to the production of services will likely accelerate with the introduction of microelectronic processes, notwithstanding the fact that microelectronic instruments are as appropriate for the production of services as they are for the production of goods. The focus of employer–employee relations and the associated legal, social, political and economic problems will continue to shift from the goods-producing commercial environment to the services-producing environment. The services-producing environment has two characteristics with implications for the labour–management process: one is that for the most part they are of a personal nature in both production and consumption, and as such are subject to social influences; and the other is that a very large proportion of the services are public and semi-public services, which are subject to political influences and decisions. Notwithstanding the efforts in recent years of certain governments, the United States and Great Britain being on the forefront, to reduce government involvement in production of goods and services and in the regulation of private sector activities, the increasing shift in employment to service activities will involve the political process increasingly in employer-employee relations.

7 On Strike Activity

INTRODUCTION

It is well to emphasise at the outset that strikes are not anti-social, nor are they incompatible with private enterprise, market economic systems. On the contrary, they are manifestations of economic and social action in free societies, and a demonstration of an important tenet of private enterprise, which is, the pursuit of self-interest.[1] In the context of the social, business and institutional environment which values tolerance of dissent and the pursuit of self-interest, the imposition of restrictions on any individual or group of individuals from exercising their freedom, without similar restrictions on other individuals and groups should be viewed discriminatory, anti-social and non-democratic. If the actions of organised employees in pursuit of their self-interest were to be limited in order to minimise the cost on enterprises and society at large, then the actions of other organisations, including business organisations, taken in pursuit of their self-interests, must be assessed from the same standpoint, and similarly limited. If the general social interest dictates the prohibition of strikes in some economic and social activities, equity considerations would dictate that the same social interest criteria be applied to all organisations which in pursuit of their self-interest impose costs on society at large. From an economic standpoint, a strike can be viewed as the withholding in supply of human services because of failure to agree on the price for those services. In substance, this is not much different from the withholding in supply of goods and services from the market or the refusal to supply a potential buyer because the demand price is less than the supply price. In the commercial world failures in negotiations for the purchase and sale of materials, goods, services, and commercial paper are common. Yet, they are not regarded negatively. Why has our society developed a negative attitude towards failures in the negotiation of agreements involving the sale and purchase of labour services?

The critical issue is not whether strikes should be permitted in a free society; the critical issue is under what conditions can a free society violate its fundamental principles of tolerance of dissent and the pursuit of self-interest by individuals, business organisations, and organised groups. A society to remain free must identify the conditions which justify social intervention and then limit its intervention to those occasions only in which the identified conditions exist. It is easier to prohibit than to tolerate. But, in a free society, it is more difficult to justify prohibition than to justify tolerance. Pressures for prohibition are for the most part manifestations of self-interest – the self-interest of political groups, the self-interest of social organisations, and the self-interest of commercial establishments. Prohibitions are for the most part violations of fundamental social principles, serving the self-interest of such groups and organisations, not the interests of society at large.

THE MAGNITUDE OF STRIKE ACTIVITY

References to strikes commonly emphasise the number of strikes, the numbers of workers involved, and the number of man-days of work lost. When examined in themselves, these loom large. Consider, for example, the case of Canada, a country whose record of strikes has been amongst the highest in the world: more than 1000 strikes in 1980, involving directly about 440 000 workers, and the loss of close to nine million man-days of work. But, when examined in relation to the total volume of activity in society and the economy, the numbers become infinitesimal: the 440 000 workers involved in strike activity represented only 4.1 per cent of the total number of workers that were employed in 1980; and the nine million man-days of work lost represents only 0.38 per cent of the total number of man-days that were worked in 1980.[2] The number of man-days of work lost because of strikes is a fraction of the man-days lost because of involuntary unemployment, illness, inclement weather, absenteeism and other causes. For example, in the week ending 20 September 1980,

865 000 workers were listed as *unemployed*
14 000 lost the entire week because of *bad weather*
163 000 lost the entire week because of *illness*
57 000 lost the entire week for *other reasons*.

Only 28 000 are recorded[3] to have lost the entire week because of *industrial disputes*.

In addition to those who lost the entire work week,

88 000 lost part of the week because of *bad weather*
256 000 lost part of the week because of *illness*
158 000 lost part of the week for *other reasons*

Only 13 000 lost part of the week because of *industrial disputes*.

Take any week through the year, and the record will most likely show that the man-days lost to industrial disputes are a fraction of the man-days lost to other causes. Why then so much emphasis on the man-days lost to strike activity, and their cost to the economy in terms of lost outputs? The evidence clearly suggests that in the context of the total man-days lost to other causes, the man-days lost to industrial disputes warrant no more than passing reference.

On the face of this reality, the agitation that is commonly associated with strike activity must be attributed to (a) the self-interest of employers whose enterprises are struck, (b) the act itself or the act of a group of employees deciding to withdraw their services from the employer until such time as acceptable terms and conditions of employment are offered, (c) the collective demonstration of the decision, often manifested in picketing of the employer's premises, and (d) the inconveniences that some strikes inflict on the public. If it were possible to construct an agitation index, the highest values will probably be recorded for disputes involving breweries, the postal service, schools, and hospitals, in that order – a manifestation of the self-interests, preferences and values of reporters and their employers, the inconvenience imposed on people accustomed to communication via the postal medium, and the inconvenience imposed on parents whose schedules are disrupted by children at home who should be at school. The economic costs of unemployment and of other developments that cause disruptions in work activity and participation in work, exceed by far the economic costs of industrial disputes.

RELATIONSHIP BETWEEN ORGANISATION AND STRIKE ACTIVITY

The number of strikes, and the number of workers involved in strike activity are related to the "populations" from which strikes originate, which is, *the number of organisations* engaged in bargaining, and *the number of workers* over whom the organisations have jurisdiction (whether they are members or not).[4] Although strikes have taken place in quest of organisation, which means before the establishment of organisation, and some spontaneous walkouts by non-organised workers have taken place in protest of some injustices, *a close relationship will be found between the number of strikes and the number of organisations engaged in collective bargaining.*[5]

It should be emphasised that in the relationship between strikes and the number of employee organisations, *the purpose* of the employee organisations is critical: the relationship will not be found with all kinds of employee organisations; it will be found rather with those organisations only formed specifically for the purpose of collective bargaining. Few strikes will be found involving nurses, doctors, engineers, policemen, firemen, airline pilots, until each of them became organised for the purpose of negotiating some terms and conditions related to the rendering of their services. Many of them had been organised for professional purposes over long periods of time; but it is the organisation for bargaining terms and conditions in the rendering of services that created the proper environment for strike activity. It is as if organising for bargaining purposes predisposes participants to strike action; it provides participants with an opportunity to vent their frustrations about the terms under which they render services and the conditions under which they perform their work functions.

Organisation for bargaining tends to institutionalise the adversarial process, it tends to centralise and perpetuate grievances, and creates an environment of conflict. Individuals tend to let conflicts die; particularly when the conflicts are resolved to their satisfaction. Organisations tend to expand the scope of conflicts, generalise from them, and use them to agitate, regardless whether they were resolved to the advantage of the workers. Organisations emphasise the struggle, the sacrifice, the effort; beneficial outcomes are made conditional on continuing agitation, continuing struggle, and continuing sacrifices. They institutionalise the process of bargaining; formalise the bargaining procedures; centralise all variables that bear on the relationship between their members and those who pay for their services; and formalise all working relationships.

VARIABLES BEARING ON THE PROPENSITY TO STRIKE

The relationship between strikes and the organisation of employees for bargaining purposes discussed in the section above refers to a relationship, not to the variables which contribute to the propensity to strike. In this section our attention focuses on that issue.

A number of variables assumed to contribute to the propensity by employees to strike have been tested, but there is no agreement amongst researchers on their relative significance:[6] one researcher, David Snyder, examined United States data on strike activity and concluded that economic factors did not bear significantly on strike activity before 1945; quest for union organisation and political developments were considerably more important. Other researchers, such as P. K. Edwards, and Jack W. Skeels, concluded that economic factors have been much more important determinants than organisational activity and political developments over the entire pre-1949 period, although occasionally within the period there will be found instances when non-economic variables had significant influences. For Canada, John Vanderkamp found mixed results. He concluded that economic conditions had a relatively weak influence on strike activity.[7] On the other hand, John D. Walsh found the *frequency of strikes* in the period 1952–72 was closely related to economic conditions.[8] But he too, found the relationship between economic activity and the duration of strikes (man-days lost) and the average number of workers involved "weak and inconsistent".[9] It is significant, however, that the strongest relationship was found to exist between price inflation and strike activity. Walsh states: "price inflation appears to be a key determinant of strike activity".[10] An examination of strike activity in the United Kingdom over the period 1893–1971 lead to the conclusion that there, too, economic conditions were the primary causal factor.[11]

The foregoing comments are not intended to be a rejection of the non-economic explanations of strike activity. There are forces in the labour-management relationship which cannot be put to statistical measurement and cannot be tested empirically. It can be argued, however, that although much strike activity can be associated with organisational drives and quests for change in employee-management relationships, the decisions of workers to respond to the call of their leaders may have been motivated by economic considerations. Although organisation or recognition of the organisation for bargaining purposes may have been the emotional factors that initiated and sustained strike activity, to the average worker staying on strike over prolonged periods the justification may well have been an *expectation* of improved economic terms of employment and working conditions. The historical record indicates that organisation was seldom put forth as an end in itself: it has always been propagated and undertaken for the purpose of improving the economic terms of employment and the conditions of work. Similarly, there is no evidence of strike action because of refusal by management to recognise the union organisation and bargain with union representatives. There is evidence of strike action because of refusal by management to negotiate a contract on terms and conditions of employment with union representatives. Is the strike action in such cases over recognition, or is it over the refusal to negotiate improvements in terms and conditions of employment *with union representatives*?

Examples also abound of strikes that have been categorised as largely political: strikes against a government's economic, social or foreign policies; strikes against war; strikes against particular pieces of labour legislation; strikes against wage and price controls. But, even in relation to such strike activity, although the motivation of the leaders may have been somewhat political, the arguments presented to workers have been largely economic – threat to freedom to bargain collectively which will ultimately bear down on their wages; increase in the power of management; exploitation of the working class; and such other. An examination of the motivations of workers who participated in such "political" strikes will determine that large majorities of them responded to the calls of their leaders on the understanding and the expectation that the outcome would be to their economic advantage – that wages will increase, hours of work will decrease, holiday periods will increase, unilateral powers of supervisory personnel will decrease, working conditions will improve. A strike cannot be categorised "political" on the ground that it is directed against government policies: strikes for the purpose of causing governments to enact legislation that would facilitate attainment of objectives related to terms of employment and working conditions or to repeal legislation that has impeded the attainment of such objectives, are well known. But, such strikes are manifestations of strategy, not of political objective. They are manifestations of deliberate decisions to seek the attainment of economic objectives through legislative enactment instead of through the one-to-one bargaining process with employers.[12]

Implicit in the foregoing is the conclusion that regardless of the nature of institutional arrangements – existence or non-existence of organisation, formalised bargaining processes and contractual relationships – most strike activity can be ascribed largely to economic considerations: workers concluding that withdrawal of their services is the only action that would bring the improvements in economic terms of employments and working conditions to which they feel entitled, and employers concluding that it is the only action which would convince workers that their demands are unattainable.

This suggests a reality that is often forgotten: *a strike is not a decision by workers to withdraw their services; it is also a decision by management to allow that to happen. A strike is not a union decision; it is a mutual decision by the union and management.* It is the manifestation of a conclusion by the union that it cannot attain its goals without strike action, and a decision by management to allow the strike to take place rather than satisfy the outstanding union demands.

It suggests also two other important realities: one is that decisions to allow a strike to take place are influenced by the degree of difference in the final positions of the respective parties, as viewed by each of them; and the other is the interpretation that each party puts to the prevailing, and anticipated, economic conditions. The common expectation in relation to the first is that the narrower the gap dividing the parties or the fewer the issues in dispute the greater the likelihood that the parties would wish to avoid a strike.[13] But, oftentimes strikes have been allowed to take place, even though the differences appeared to be very narrow indeed. Which suggests other influences, such as different perceptions by the parties of the importance of outstanding issues; inadequate or imperfect analyses of the issues; inadequate or imperfect communication between the parties; or a conclusion by either party that prevailing and anticipated economic conditions promise an outcome after the strike that is more advantageous than that to be achieved without a strike.

In the context of the above, variations over time in the labour–management relations environment from one of high agitation to one of tranquility must be ascribed to the interpretation by the respective parties of prevailing and anticipated economic conditions, the formulation of their respective programmes, and the response of each to the other's programme. Neither party can be cited as entirely or largely responsible for the resulting environment: responsibility rests with both. An environment of high agitation could result as much from "unrealistic" union demands as from "unrealistic" management responses to demands. Martin J. Mauro argues: "the probability of a strike occurring will increase if one party bases its perception of the opponent's position on the same variables employed to form its own position, when the opponent's position is, in fact, based on different variables".[14]

The foregoing does not deny the fact that strikes have taken place in quest of power, both in relation to management and in relation to intra-union and inter-union leadership struggles. What better way for a determined union leader to show the strength of leadership than to wage a successful battle against management. Indeed, it would be totally unrealistic to assume that labour and management have always entered the bargaining process rationally, and engaged in the game of give-and-take after careful calculations of the advantages and disadvantages, costs and benefits of alternative actions. Emotions, frustrations, interpersonal likes and dislikes, political philosophies, personal aspirations, and scores of other non-economic considerations influence the outcomes of bargaining processes. But, the strikes that can be attributed to such causes have been the exceptions, not the rule.

COST OF STRIKES

Strikes are costly to both employees and enterprises: employees lose income and often jobs as well, whereas enterprises suffer losses in productivity over varying periods before and after a strike, lose trained employees to competitors, incur penalties for failures to meet contractual obligations with suppliers and buyers, and incur costs in efforts to regain lost sales. It is estimated that in the United States such costs have varied between $200 per man-day for small enterprises with 100 or fewer production employees, and $300 per man-day for enterprises with 500 to 1000 production employees.[15]

Yet, strikes can be prevented. Like accidents, fires, and other man-made occurrences they can be avoided[16] – a fact attested to by enterprises that have never been struck, which is most enterprises, everywhere. It can be presumed that in most enterprises employees and management have considered the costs and benefits that would accrue to each from agreement with and without strike action, and concluded that on balance peaceful co-existence entails lesser costs and greater benefits than periodic warfare.

It is often the case in strike situations that such calculations of costs and benefits do not take place. Instead, emotions are allowed to govern rationale: existing precedents and the possible establishment of precedents are allowed to interfere with discussions on viable alternatives; legal maneuverings are allowed to exasperate the parties to the bargaining process; accustomed managerial and work practices are allowed to become inflexible barriers; union demands are interpreted to threaten management prerogatives; management responses to union demands are interpreted to threaten established work practices; management decides "to teach the union a lesson"; the union decides "to have it out once and for all".

The more one examines individual conflicts and the issues that ultimately lead to them, the more one becomes convinced of their economic irrationality. Which suggests that few strikes will stand the test of economic rationality, either for the employees who go out and stay out, or for management who allow them to take place and agree implicitly to their continuation over time. Although the underlying reasons may be predominantly economic, more often than not strikes are the result of unsatisfactory work environments, adversarial relationships between management and officers of employee organisations, unsatisfactory supervision of work and work processes, and management styles which do not allow for consultations prior to measures that effect employees adversely – heavy costs to bear for deficiencies in organisation and human relations.

THE INFLUENCE OF PUBLIC OPINION ON DISPUTES AND DISPUTE–SETTLEMENT[17]

"Industrial conflict", wrote A. W. R. Carrothers, "is a political event in which each contestant seeks to marshall public opinion in its favour, even though in the occasional dispute either side may profess its indifference to, or contempt for the moral force of public opinion. Further, in a dispute in the public sector, where a profit motive does not supply leverage for settlement, public opinion may have to be an initial sanction."[18] How much influence does public opinion have on relations between labour and management and in the settlement of disputes between them? Are they influenced by what is reported through the media or by what they each determine to be the prevailing view of the public? Which public? Without doubt the parties have different publics or place different weights on the opinions of different groups of the public.

Since labour–management disputes affect different groups of the public differently, it may be appropriate to divide the public into two groups: participants and outsiders.[19] In the "participants" group would be included those members of the public who are affected by the dispute, such as, users of the goods and services produced by the disputants, producers and users of goods and services whose production depends on the goods and services of the disputants, members of the families of disputants, workers laid off because of the dispute and their families, and those who sell to the disputants and to others whose incomes have been affected. The extent to which users will be effected and the extent to which they will press for a speedy settlement, will depend, of course, on the extent to which alternative sources of supply are available at the same price and with the same convenience.[20]

In the "outsiders" group would be included those members of the public who are not affected by the dispute, whether directly or indirectly, and who therefore, could not have any interest in the outcome of the dispute. To the extent that this group registers an opinion it may be motivated by moral, social and political considerations, rather than economic considerations or considerations related to the terms and conditions of work and relations between the disputing parties. In such case, the question arises whether or to what extent should the parties take note of the opinions expressed by the group.

Workers have always had a strong reservation about the nature and strength of public opinion: they have often expressed displeasure at what they believe to be unfair and inaccurate reporting by the media, which allegedly misinforms the public and creates a biased public opinion; secondly, there has always existed a question about whose opinion is being communicated – the opinion prevailing amongst participant groups or the opinion of the outsider groups. Since the latter have traditionally had easier access to media instruments, there has always existed a suspicion that their opinion predominated. Thirdly, there has always prevailed a view amongst workers that the media are either controlled or influenced by their employers, and that therefore, they should always expect an effort by them to bias public opinion in favour of the employer; and finally, since the public is not directly affected by many of the issues in dispute, it could not be expected that the public will appreciate fully the need for the strong stand workers occasionally take.[21]

These are legitimate reservations and concerns. But, in many instances the workers themselves are misinformed or inadequately informed: the nature of information they are given by their organisations on the terms and conditions of employment offered by employers, the methods and manner in which the information is given, and presentations on relations with employers and governments, are often designed to alienate rather than illuminate. The motives differ from instance to instance: inexperienced and insecure leadership; dictatorial leadership using the big lie method; politically motivated leadership; control of the organisation by agitators, serving special interests; and many other. Inadequate and inaccurate information, and the methods and manner in which information is communicated, introduce preconceived biases in the decision-making process, and stack the cards in favour of those who control the production and distribution of the information.[22] To those who accept the information as being accurate and representative of the true situation, all other information is biased, and public opinion formulated on the basis of such biased information is by implication itself biased. This sort of reasoning makes the rejection of public opinion a justifiable option.

But, such reservations, suspicions, and alleged or established deficiencies in the system are a natural consequence of freedom and diversity. Their existence should not be interpreted to manifest a general disregard of public opinion. If public opinion did not matter in the conduct of labour-management relations, then the parties would not engage in efforts designed to influence it; yet, both of them allocate considerable time, effort and resources in pronouncements and advertisements designed to make the public understand and appreciate the "reasonableness" of their respective positions. In all probability, strikes in the public sector, particularly those of teachers, nurses, postmen, railway workers, non-medical hospital workers, and such other, would have lasted longer than they did, but for the force of public opinion. Similarly, decisions by governments to order or to seek court orders for the termination of strikes can be regarded as responses to public pressure.

Perhaps the most telling demonstration of the influence of public opinion on the parties and on governments is what happens in the absence of clearly formulated public opinion: disputes tend to drag on and governments adopt a hands-off policy, regardless of the nature of service provided by the disputants. Presumably, if the public can do without the service over a prolonged period of time, or if the public can find partial or full substitutes for the service, even though costly and less convenient, it may become indifferent and let the dispute drag on. An example of this is provided by the October–November 1975 strike of the Canadian Union of Postal Workers. Over a period of five years preceding the strike, the postal service was interrupted so frequently, and had become so erratic and unreliable, that the public developed a rather cynical attitude towards it. Government efforts to improve it through automation and the introduction of a postal code were being frustrated by the Canadian Union of Postal Workers, which had embarked upon a policy of confrontation and boycott. The long period of negotiation that preceded the strike was accompanied by pronouncements, threats and warnings from the union that a strike was inevitable unless the government gave in to its demands. The public was prepared to accept the strike and when the strike came it surprised no one. Indeed, as the strike dragged on, the public seemed to develop a sense of indifference towards it, which contributed to its continuation. Had there been an outcry instead, the strike would have been terminated sooner, either by negotiation or compulsory arbitration. It can be concluded, therefore, that public opinion can contribute to the shortening or lengthening of disputes, depending on whether it is respectively strongly negative or indifferent.

What would cause the public to become indifferent to a dispute? The availability of alternative sources of the struck goods and services and the availability of substitutes would be one reason; another would be the availability of alternative sources of income for the workers involved in the dispute, and for workers affected by the dispute – earnings of other family members, strike pay, unemployment insurance, welfare, savings, loans; and still another would be lack of adequate information. The amount and nature of information made available to the public about individual disputes is frequently so inadequate as to preclude the possibility of forming an informed public opinion. Even on major disputes, the issues are not given the degree of detailed and widespread publicity that would be necessary for the expression of public opinion. The information that is commonly given relates to some of the major issues, such as the question of automation, the question of part-time workers, the question of over-time, the question of pay, but not the nature of difficulties encountered in reaching an agreement. The public cannot be expected to form an opinion on what would constitute a reasonable basis for settlement, without information on the nature of positions taken by the parties and the nature of arguments the parties present in support of their respective positions.

If public opinion were to have a strong influence in the settlement of labour-management disputes, the public would have to be given access to all information that relates to the disputes – profits, prices, productivity, costs, competition, restrictive practices, comparative wages and other terms and conditions of employment. The target audience would be the public at large, users of the goods and services produced by the disputants, suppliers of goods and services to the disputants, and members of the disputing organisations – workers, managers, professional or other non-organised employees, and shareholders. The most effective publicity would be provided, of course, by open forum investigations: let the parties argue the merits of their positions and let the public determine what would constitute a reasonable basis for settlement. "For Public Opinion to be effective" wrote MacKenzie King, "it is necessary that it be made an informed Opinion." This is why he put the emphasis on the investigative role of the conciliation process. He believed that if conciliation boards were to examine and comment on profits, and prices as well as on wages, the result would be "an intelligently formed Public Opinion".[23]

THIRD PARTIES AND PUBLIC OPINION

The involvement of third parties in the settlement of labour–management disputes is based on two expectations: one is that neutrality will result in an unbiased examination of the issues in dispute and recommendations acceptable to both parties, and the other is that neutrality will influence public opinion which in turn will influence the response of the parties to the recommendations. MacKenzie King wrote: "It is not to be supposed that, because findings of Compulsory Investigation are not enforceable under penalty, findings in such cases are without effect. Public Opinion, as an instrument of authority, may be more subtle and elusive than the power of Law visualised in penalties and prisons."[24]

The reactions of employee organisations to the outcomes of third party involvement have been generally favourable. Occasionally some have demonstrated contempt for both the recommendations of third parties and public opinion, manifested in illegal strikes, and defiance of court orders and orders of legislatures, but such are exceptions. In the context of the totality of labour-management contractual relationships, and in the context of the number of disputes settled on the basis of third party recommendations or as a result of third party involvement, manifestations of contempt are very few indeed.

The historical record suggests that strikes, with varying degrees of violence and illegality, are a periodic phenomenon in our society. Perhaps we need such behavioural manifestations from time to time as a sort of catharsis in social relations and in relations between labour and management. It is perhaps necessary to the development and long run stability of our democratic processes and institutions to challenge from time to time established and seemingly accepted rules, regulations, processes and procedures. Challenges compel the re-examination of the fundamental premises on which rules, regulations and procedures are based.

Workers who have participated in illegal strikes and engaged in some violent activities have viewed their actions as necessary challenges to rules, regulations and conditions which appeared to them unfair and unjust. Frequently they become agitated by what they believe to be unfair treatment from their employers, unduly restrictive legislation, unwarranted injunctions handed down by biased judges, and occasionally by a leadership lacking experience and courage. They know that public opinion would not favour their actions, but can find no alternative ways to express forcefully their growing frustrations.

WORKER DISCONTENT

Most pronouncements on worker discontent as a cause of labour–management disputes are based on the fundamental premise that the contemporary blue-collar worker is younger and better educated than his predecessors, he has a broader perspective of society, the world of work, and his role in it;[25] he is not satisfied with a system of values which in his view place an undue degree of emphasis on work, nor is he satisfied with the social and organisational structure of the work-place; hence, he seeks a more meaningful form of participation in the work process – one which will restore to him his identity, which allegedly he has lost in the modern, large, impersonal industrial and institutional enterprise. While striving for change he remains alienated, ever ready to strike at any moment, with little or no concern about efficiency, productivity and, indeed, the survival of such enterprises.

This may be an accurate description of the nature of change that has taken place over time in the composition of the labour force and in the attitudes of some workers, but the indicated reasons for the change in attitudes remain to be tested. It so happens, for example, that worker discontent has often co-incided with rising unemployment, rising prices, falling pro-ductivity, and substantial improvements in social security payments, and was often just preceded by an unprecedented period of rising real incomes. It is well known that as incomes rise above subsistence people begin to make choices between pecuniary and non-pecuniary returns for their services. It should not be surprising, therefore, that as incomes rise workers would be asking for improvements in working conditions, more mean-ingful relationships between worker and work environment, longer holidays, and other non-monetary rewards.

To the extent that employers fail to appreciate such a change in preferences and fail to make appropriate satisfactory pro-visions for improvement in working conditions, the reaction of workers may well be dissatisfaction even though substantial pay improvements may be granted. On the other hand, it is conceiv-able that employers do appreciate the change in preferences but fail to carry out improvements in working conditions and resort to the payment of high wages as a trade-off for improved con-ditions.[26] However, higher wages increase the expectation of enjoyment of both work and leisure; in the absence of improve-ments in working conditions, and in the absence of longer holidays, the higher pay is likely to increase rather than reduce the intensity of discontent.

The evidence that manifestations of discontent have coincided with substantial improvements in social security payments war-rants some attention. As social security payments rise, and access to them becomes more liberal, the importance of work as a means of subsistence diminishes; and when subsistence can be had without work, then one can afford to be selective in the nature of work one undertakes. In this context, expressions of disaffection with the value system, disagreement with the work ethic, and dissatisfaction with the worker–work relationship and the work environment, are mere manifestations of the opportu-nity afforded by easy access to social security subsistence to choose between work and leisure.

People who get no pleasure from their work, and who find no other need for it except the income they get from it, may be expected to quit when alternative sources of income are made available to them.

CHANGING AGE DISTRIBUTION OF THE LABOUR FORCE

Frequent reference has been made in recent years to the changing age composition of the labour force as a factor contributing to the increase in labour–management disputes. It is alleged that the proportion of young workers in the labour force has been increasing, and their influence on union policies has been rising. Since the young are less patient, less tolerant and have less regard for traditional relationships and practices than do older workers, their influence is perceived to be disruptive.

The question is whether the increase in the proportion of young workers was substantial enough to influence decision-making within union organisations. A few more loud voices always help, particularly in situations where the majority either do not participate at all or accept passively whatever is proposed. But, although the real force of the influence may emanate from young workers, it is not necessarily related to the higher proportion of young workers in the labour force. Rather, it may be related to the fact that workers generally are more knowledgeable of society, the economy, social and political institutions, and participate more actively than did workers ten or more years ago.

In the past, age, experience and authority were barriers to communication: they impeded the effective participation of workers. Now those barriers have largely been lifted; and workers feel freer to express their opinions. The rank-and-file have become more visible: they are no longer reluctant to face older, more experienced union officials and question the effectiveness of their methods in dealing with management; they are not reluctant to face management with proposals on terms and conditions of employment that differ significantly from traditional "packages"; and they are not reluctant to question the necessity or reasonableness of rules and regulations. These are the developments that have made workers generally more influential in union policy-making and labour–management relations, not the numbers of young workers in the labour force.

CHANGING PERSONAL, OCCUPATIONAL AND SOCIAL VALUES

Related to the above comments in the evidence of changes in personal, occupational and social values generally.[27] In the past, many workers were governed in their occupational behaviour by traditional codes, the strict observance of which was a condition of employment. To some of them, wages, hours of work and conditions of work rated relatively low in their value systems: a sense of duty and dedication to service exceeded by far all other considerations. Potential sources of conflict with management were more likely to relate to physical and other impediments to the rendering of high quality service, than to monetary and other inducements for the rendering of high quality service.

It was generally assumed that those who sought preparation as nurses, teachers, social workers, clergy and such other occupations; those who entered employments which provided services to the ill, the poor, the handicapped and generally what might be called health and social services; and many of those who entered public service employments, were motivated by expectations other than income and comfortable working conditions. They were cast in desirable social roles – martyrs, angels of mercy, mothers – and were expected to render services to society at large, to those who could not look after themselves, to the underprivileged, and to suffer in the process as a matter of individual choice, social responsibility and duty. The personal satisfaction that they received, which was assumed to be considerable, was viewed as partial compensation ("psychic income") to be supplemented with compensation for physical sustenance and comfort, in the form usually of food, shelter, clothing and some token monetary income.

It is relevant to note that these expectations did not extend to the higher levels of occupational and managerial (administrative) categories of employment in the indicated activities. While they were largely instrumental in the perpetuation of the myth of psychic income, few of them indicated themselves any readiness to take part of their relatively high incomes in the form of personal satisfaction. It is a manifestation of the prevailing social structure, inter-occupational relationships, and employer–employee relations that those who occupy higher level positions feel themselves competent to determine the degree of personal satisfaction that others should derive from the occupational services they render. Employees at the lower levels of the occupational or employment structure were expected to trade-off part of their potential wages for the privilege of having certain occupational designations or for the privilege of being associated in employment with certain high level individuals, families or establishments.[28]

The myth of psychic income became so well entrenched in the pay systems of social institutions as to cause in recent times some serious conflicts in labour–management relations. Management (administrators) resisted recognition and acceptance of the proposition that dedication to one's work, pride in one's work and satisfaction from one's work, should be rewarded and not deducted from the potential earnings of the employees involved. Like the ancient Greeks, they lost the capacity to distinguish between mythology and reality, and thereby fostered an environment conducive to conflict. There emerged relatively wide disparities in payments, not only between comparable occupational and employment classifications amongst institutions and establishments, but also between occupations and employment classifications within individual institutions, depending upon whether or not occupations and employments were deemed to derive "psychic income" from their service activities.

Values have changed. There was a time not long ago when relatively low paid employees in the social services (including hospital employees), were resisting efforts to organise them for collective bargaining purposes, even though they were presented with convincing evidence that they were disadvantaged relative to other employments and occupations. But, they seemed satisfied with their work, with their contributions to whatever was being done, and did not seem too concerned about the fact that they were being exploited. This attitude of beneficence has gradually disappeared. Increasingly employees who perform necessary, socially valuable and essential services demand compensation that reflects the social value, the necessity and the essentiality of the service. Postmen, hospital workers, garbage collectors, transportation workers, teachers and many other such employees have expressed themselves in such terms.

A contributing factor to the change in attitudes of such employees was the widening gap in wages and salaries between themselves and administrative and professional employees within their own establishments. Although in many instances the gap may have been imposed by the market, (i.e. the increasing scarcity of competent administrative and professional employees), to the general body of hospital, municipal, postal, educational, and other workers it appeared inconsistent with claims of inability to pay, calls for restraint, and consideration of the public interest. Teachers could not understand why administrators within the system, whose educational qualifications were the same as their own, were paid twice or more the average teacher salary; nurses, particularly those with four or five-year university degrees, could not understand why physicians with one or two more years of schooling than themselves were being paid four or five times more; postmen, who believe themselves to be performing a valuable public service, could not understand why the pay gap between themselves and administrators appeared to be widening, and why administrators had employment security while they were exposed to the vicissitudes of the market and changes in technology. Comparisons of this nature generate agitation, because there are no generally acceptable answers. Even if there were agreement that salary differentials between teachers and superintendents, doctors and nurses, postmen and administrators were justifiable and necessary, the amount of the differential could not be determined scientifically, and remained a source of conflict.

When employees accept the evidence of inability to pay or agree to restrain their demands so that some aspect of the national interest will be attained – to stabilise the price level, to reduce unemployment, to strengthen the competitive position in foreign markets – they expect similar responses from other employees, and particularly from those who are higher in the occupational and salary structure. Any evidence that others have gained while they restrained creates an environment of distrust and conflict.

In this context, it should not be surprising that there has prevailed in recent years an environment of conflict in both Western Europe and North America: calls for restraint were in many instances not heeded by those who called for restraint; and inability to pay did not seem to effect the increases granted to higher level occupational classifications. One cannot expect the masses to behave responsibly, when the behaviour of industrial, political, social and institutional leaders casts doubt on the wisdom of responsible behaviour. If by heeding the call for restraint and behaving responsibly some employees become disadvantaged relative to other employees, they would be bearing a cost burden not shared by others. Only individuals whose personal values regarding work, pay, social status, and related issues differ from the social norm are likely to accept such a development. But, to the extent that such variances in values are incidental, acts and responses of leaders and other groups in society that depart from guidelines propagated by the leaders, will generate agitation and conflict.

WORKER LOYALTY AND EMPLOYER FAIRNESS

There prevails a general view that loyalty to companies, institutions, systems and organisations has declined significantly over the past two or three decades, and that it continues to decline. Only very long service employees appear to demonstrate some partiality towards their employers, but even amongst them increasing numbers have been expressing doubts about the sense of fairness of modern management towards their employees.

The majority of workers cannot understand how one could or why one should develop a sense of loyalty towards employers, companies or institutions; nor can they appreciate the nature of employer–employee relationships that existed in the distant past which resulted in the degree of loyalty expressed by some long service and retired workers. The senior officer of a large labour organisation whose father and grandfather retired from the company with which he is now employed himself, and whose representatives he meets at the bargaining table, finds his father's attitude perplexing. Apparently, he is often scolded for being too critical of company policies, even when the criticism relates to the very low pension that his father receives after forty-five years of service to the company. Another union officer who is employed by the same company expressed the opinion that the attitude of management towards their employees has changed: he believes management at all levels were more production oriented in the past, and since production was highly labour intensive, they demonstrated concern for their workers and even for the workers' families. It was common to find companies discriminating in favour of sons, daughters and relatives of their employees in hiring, and as a result it was common for grandfathers, fathers and sons to be employed in the same company. The workers, in turn, developed a sense of trust in the company and a feeling that the company will be fair in its treatment of the workers. Disputes arose, in some instances frequently and heatedly, but they were in the nature of family disputes. Now there is a different environment: increasing capitalisation and accompanying changes in organisational structures shifted the attention and concern of management away from their workers. Furthermore, most managers are now professional managers, not owner–employers. Their view of employees is as factors of production, not as their workers.

The negative attitudes of workers are not limited to management and the enterprises that employ them; they extend to their own organisations and their leaders. The increasing tendency of workers to reject or nearly reject agreements submitted by their union leaders for ratification manifests their alienation. Many workers view their own organisations from the same perspective as they view the firms for which they work – insiders on the outside, facing bureaucratic administrative structures staffed by indifferent officials who communicate through memoranda or stare occasionally from behind massive desks or from raised platforms. They are equally officious, equally patronising, equally concerned about their organisations, and equally distrustful of the motives, goals and aspirations of individual workers and groups of workers.

It is conceivable, of course, that manifestations of loyalty to employers, and support of employee organisations and leaders in the past were motivated by self-interest. Jobs were not very plentiful prior to the 1940s and good jobs were very scarce. Losing one's job involved prolonged periods of search, loss of all income (since unemployment insurance either did not exist or employment qualifications were too long or waiting periods were too long or payments were relatively small), and often necessitated geographic relocation. It is natural, therefore, that those who were fortunate to find good jobs for themselves and their close relatives should profess loyalty towards their employers as protection against the large numbers of actual and potential competitors.

In the recent decades of unprecedented economic growth and full employment there has developed a sense of employment security; and the considerable improvement in unemployment insurance and other forms of social security has removed the total dependence on employment as a means of subsistence. Despite the periodic declines in economic activity and the accompanying increase in unemployment, and despite the rather significant changes in the structure of the economy and the accompanying displacement of workers, the growth of the economy on the aggregate has given workers, particularly younger workers, a sense of optimism regarding their ability to find good jobs and earn a relatively good standard of living.

This sense of economic security and optimism has given workers the courage to resist the introduction of measures, practices and processes that are motivated by efficiency alone. They have come to view with scepticism the quest for efficiency and cost effectiveness, and are asking questions about social costs, human values, and social benefits to workers and consumers. Few workers would today accept passively the introduction of new processes, and most are likely to demonstrate increasing resistance to processes which tend to deprive them of the limited opportunities that they have for personal judgement, association, discourse and interaction with fellow workers. To the extent that they are not able to prevent the introduction of measures which affect them adversely they absent themselves from work more frequently, demand longer vacations, shorter hours per day and week, longer coffee breaks, recreation facilities, and early retirement with substantial pension. The argument that management knows best, which was commonplace and generally accepted by workers up to about the 1950s, is now rejected outright. Even management's claim to better knowledge on what is in the interest of the firm is being increasingly challenged. Management must recognise that employees at all levels of the occupational structure may be as informed on many general economic, social, political and institutional issues as themselves. Platitudes, patronisations and pontifications have no effect on them. Increasing levels of education have stimulated quests for information on the purposes of their employment, for opportunities to participate in the decision-making process on matters that effect the conduct of their work, and for opportunities to participate in the making of choices amongst alternative forms of terms and conditions of employment.[29] The vertical decision-making process to which management has been accustomed will have to give way to a horizontal model, especially in relation to decisions that relate to methods of employment and terms and conditions of employment.[30]

8 Technology and Employment Issues[1]

INTRODUCTION

Technology bargaining will become a critical issue in the late 1980s and will intensify through the 1990s, when computers and telecommunications technology converge into microelectronic networks, and impact severely on organisational structures, processes, products, occupations and employment. Given rapid economic growth, the associated problems will be largely problems of adjustment only; but, in the absence of adequate growth relative to the growth in the labour force, the problem of inadequate employment opportunities will be added to the adjustment problems. Whether the problems are adjustment problems only, or they are adjustment and employment problems, they concern employees and their organisations; and as they become increasingly critical, they can be expected to be moved up the agenda for discussions with management and governments.

Considering *the nature* of on-going changes in technology, and *the rate* of technological change, it can be expected with certainty that in the 1980s and 1990s human adjustments to changes in technology and employment will become central issues in labour–management relations, the outcomes of which will depend largely on the responses of the parties to the emerging problems. Failure of the parties to resolve the emerging problems through the collective bargaining process, will result in the intervention of the legislative process.

A retrospective examination of government responses to critical issues in labour–management relations suggests that only pre-emptive measures will prevent serious conflicts. Critical issues have never been resolved satisfactorily through bargaining: ultimately the legislative process has proven more effective and more permanent in the solution of outstanding labour-management problems than the bargaining process. Although the bargaining process often initiated discussions on issues of concern to labour, the legislative process invariably stepped-in to establish minimum standards, when such standards were deemed socially desirable. Whenever social consensus could not be established, and the legislative process could not be forced to act, the outstanding issues remained outstanding – the bargaining process has not been able to resolve them. For example, issues such as advance notice to workers and their organisations on pending technological and other changes likely to have negative employment effects; consultations with worker representatives on issues of adjustment to changes in the organisation of work; retraining, relocation and re-employment of displaced workers; redundancy compensation, supplementary unemployment benefits, pensions, and such other issues that relate to employment security and risk to occupational stability and income, have been outstanding for a long time and remain outstanding in most enterprises, notwithstanding the periodic efforts of employee organisations to secure management commitments through the bargaining process. But, an examination of bargaining agendas will establish that the efforts of employee organisations have been weak and uncertain; which explains both the failure of the bargaining process to deal with them, and the failure of the legislative process to act on them. Unlike issues that relate to recognition of employee organisations for collective bargaining purposes, participation in the bargaining process in good faith, and issues that relate to employment and work, such as hours of work, overtime work and overtime pay, holidays, minimum wages, health and safety, employee organisations have not put a high priority to issues that relate to the effects of technological and other changes on employment and occupations, and to the problems of unemployed workers. Labour leaders have verbalised on the issues, but there is no evidence of high priority in the bargaining agenda.

The contents of collective agreements indicate that the collective bargaining process has had very limited success in establishing common minimum standards on those important issues. Perhaps they were not important issues heretofore, and as a result were not given priority in the bargaining agenda. But, there is no evidence of changes in bargaining priorities, notwithstanding the increase of interest and expressions of concern about the potential effects of robots and other microelectronic products, instruments and processes. The implication of all this should be clear: the legislative process must assume the initiative and establish minimum standards of responsibility towards employees who are adversely affected by technological changes. Failure to do so will shift the burden to the bargaining process, which has not proven itself effective on such issues. Furthermore, unlike the technologies of the recent past which were applied sporadically and to relatively limited industrial processes, microelectronic technologies are highly pervasive in application, which means that their effects will be widespread. It would not be prudent to rely on individual bargaining, establishment by establishment, to establish the minimum standards. A universal problem cannot be attended satisfactorily in an ad hoc, industry by industry, basis. This reality caused Britain's Trade Union Congress (TUC) to issue a policy statement urging unions to approach the issue of technological change jointly, so that technology agreements will cover the largest possible proportion of the workforce.[2]

Yet, the history of collective bargaining indicates that governments have relied on the ad hoc method to resolve universal problems: labour and management struggled long and hard over the issue of recognition of employee organisations, for example, before governments recognised the universality of the issue and established standard criteria for the recognition of organisations. It is to be hoped that such will not be the case in this instance. The problem is too urgent, and the issues are too critical, to allow their resolution through the heretofore ineffective collective bargaining process. With the widespread application of microelectronic instruments and processes, and the progressive reduction in labour intensity of products and production processes, employees will intensify their pressures on their organisations and on governments for protection against unilateral decisions that affect their livelihood, for adjustments in employment relationships to accommodate the technologies, such as the hours of work, vacations, leaves and such other, and for guarantees of employment and incomes. These are the issues of the 1990s.

TECHNOLOGICAL IMPERATIVES AND THE MANAGERIAL ETHIC

While considering appropriate common responses to negative effects on employees, employment and occupations, we must address two critical issues: one is the issue of technological determinism, and the other is the issue of the managerial ethic which holds that the employment of people is variable, adjustable and dispensable, whereas the employment of physical capital is unalterable and fixed.

In relation to the first, we must ask the question to what extent negative effects on work processes, work environments, employment and skills commonly attributed to technology are in fact dictated by the technology, and to what extent they are the result of human decisions motivated by considerations of competition and costs. And in relation to the second, we must ask the question to what extent management efficiency will be impaired if employment of the human factor were to be treated as quasi-fixed,[3] and if enterprises were to be explicitly required to allocate part of the increase in productivity associated with the changes in technology to the defrayal of the social and individuals costs associated with the changes in technology.

An examination of the evidence will probably find that many adverse effects on individuals and the environment were the result of the introduction of new technologies before they were ready for introduction, and the introduction of technologies in ways that would reduce costs of production to the enterprise, regardless of the costs that were thereby imposed on workers and society at large. This ability of enterprises to transfer potential operating costs from themselves to employees and society at large hides the real costs of technological change and gives thereby a comparative advantage to technology over labour in production processes. The question arises where would be the advantage if technology were to bear all the costs associated with its operation.

As long as enterprises are able to transfer technology-related operating costs from themselves to workers and society at large, they are not likely to make any serious effort to reduce such costs, and technology will maintain its advantage over labour in production. Considerations of efficiency in the utilisation of human and material resources dictate that each factor of production bear all costs that are associated with its employment. Only then would it be possible to determine the relative advantages of employing one factor or another. To the extent that a factor is able to shift some of the costs of its employment to other factors, it will gain an advantage over the other factors, which, of course, is deceptive in the total context. Let us take an example: in quest of operational efficiency the barriers come down at a railway crossing in the city and a train with 120 cars moves along bringing traffic to a standstill. The cars, trucks, buses and people that are idled thereby incur very considerable costs which should in fact be borne by the railway. As long as the railway is able to transfer its costs to society at large, the technology will not bear the full cost of its operation, and will thereby retain its advantage over alternative forms of conveyance. The railway will incur the full cost when it is required to construct and maintain an overpass or an underpass at that crossing. A similar analysis can be used in relation to pollution, the redundancy of skills, injuries and health impairment, and other. If enterprises were to be required to make substantial redundancy payments to displaced employees, or were to bear the full cost associated with injuries and the impairment of health, and to undertake the retraining and re-employment of redundant employees, it is most likely that they will manage their human resources more responsibly than when such employment-related effects cost them nothing. The social significance of this issue is immense: it is critical to the determination of the relative efficiencies of different forms of enterprise and to the efficient utilisation of human and material resources. In view of this, society and its various institutions, including the organisations of employees, may be deemed to have a legitimate right to inputs in decision-making processes that effect their welfare. The outstanding question on this matter is not the desirability and feasibility of such inputs; it is rather the mechanisms by which the inputs can be provided without thereby erecting barriers to the introduction of change, and without impairing the efficiency of processes.[4]

IMPLICATIONS FOR EMPLOYMENT AND UNION RESPONSES

"Industrialisation" wrote Clark Kerr and his collaborators "challenges the old hierarchy and replaces it with a new ordering of the classes; professionals, managers, administrators, and industrial workers replace the pre-industrial economic ordering of landowners, merchants and traders, master craftsmen and guild journeymen, apprentices, and peasants."[5] The evolution of the post-industrial economic order can be expected to replace the industrial economic order in effect over the past century. The industrial worker will undoubtedly be replaced by the information process worker; the nature of functions performed by professional workers – doctors, engineers, accountants – can be expected to change significantly as micro-electronic technology eliminates some of them and undertakes the performance of other; the managerial and administrative structure can be expected to change in both functions and hierarchical ordering; and the convergence of computers and telecommunications technology into telematic systems can be expected to stimulate vertical and horizontal integration of enterprises. All present occupations and employments can be expected to be effected negatively including some that are currently in high demand, such as programmers. Redundancy of knowledge, redundancy of skills, reductions in the labour intensity of production processes, the elimination of products and processes and their functionally related employments, have become accepted as technological imperatives. All these developments will impact on the organisations of workers, and on the processes by which terms and conditions of employment are set.

Almost one decade ago, Philip Taft wrote: "Unions must adapt themselves to changes in the number and quality of the labor force, technology, and the laws that govern their existence and those which regulate collective bargaining."[6] The historical record indicates that unions have never accepted the laws that governed their existence as being cast in stone. They seldom recognised them as anything more than a phase in the continuing evolution of the changing relationships with employers and governments. Therefore, whatever adaption was put into effect was generally deemed temporary – until the next change. Had unions merely accepted and adapted to the laws that governed them they would have submitted themselves to the dictates of existing political processes and those who exercised the dominant influence on them.

Unions have traditionally played an active role in the formulation, interpretation and administration of the laws that govern their existence. But, not so in relation to the formulation and implementation of decisions involving technological changes. Even though, not unlike the political and legislative processes, decisions on all aspects of technological change are taken by people, and even though the negative effects on employment and skills are most often the result of human decisions, the notion of a technological imperative propagated by employers and their engineers, appears to have been generally accepted. Acceptance dictates, of course, adaptability to whatever technological change is implemented, and removes the burden of accountability from those who take the decisions. Such outcomes suggest a technological imperative. Although there are imperatives in technological change, all effects are not technologically imperative.

History attests that resistance to technological change and withdrawal of services (railway firemen, elevator constructors, printers) or job control (apprentice-journeymen ratios, shop arrangements, production-process rules and regulations) has seldom saved any jobs. In some cases, such measures delayed the implementation of some technological changes, and put off temporarily the displacement of some workers, but they neither prevented implementation nor avoided displacement. This fact does not, of course, attest to the existence of technological imperatives, it attests to the ineffectiveness of resistance when the technology is at the implementation stage of development, and decisions have been taken to implement. If union intervention were to minimise the negative effects on employment and skills, it would have to take place at the planning stages of the technological change. The implementation stage is too late for modifications to the technology; all that can be hoped for at that stage, is to negotiate satisfactory accommodative arrangements for those who would be adversely effected.

In the context of the nature and magnitude of technological changes implemented during the past four decades, the recorded union resistance has been generally moderate. The growth of the economy and the accompanying increase in employment opportunities made such a response quite acceptable. But, unions would have been justified to protest more vigorously than they have done, particularly in relation to the widespread practice of presenting changes and their consequences in their final forms. Workers have a right to earn their livelihood, and their organisations have a responsibility to protect and safeguard their livelihood. When those who propose to deprive them of that livelihood fail to put forth programmes designed to adjust and accommodate displaced workers, all workers and their organisations are duty bound to resist.[7] Resistance in quest of employment security is resistance in defence of economic self-interest – a principle widely recognised for its legitimacy in private enterprise, market economies.

Industry does not, of course, view the relationship in such terms. To management, labour is a factor of production, purchased at a price to do a job. Employment will continue only as long as the job continues to exist. When the job is terminated, for whatever reason, the labour that did that job will no longer be needed, and, therefore, will no longer be purchased. This is the philosophy that underlies the common practice of informing the union about pending technological changes at the eleventh hour. The intent is not to tell the union about the technological change itself; it is rather to inform the union of the jobs that will be terminated, and what is to be done with the labour that was hired to do those jobs.

The practice of informing the union on the eleventh hour has had negative effects on relations between unions and management, as well as on relations between unions and their members. Workers expect to be protected against unilateral and arbitrary management measures. The fact that the union may have been informed on the eleventh hour is not a convincing argument. They want to know why the union did not make an effort to determine that technological changes were being planned. This issue will assume increasing importance as the rate of technological change accelerates, and increasing numbers of workers are effected. Officers of employee organisations will be expected to know about the nature of pending technology and its potential effects on employments and skills, and will be expected to negotiate satisfactory accommodative arrangements before the implementation stage. Failure to be informed until actual implementation, and having to negotiate accommodative arrangements under duress, are signs of weakness in leadership.

UNION ATTITUDES CLASSIFIED

A United States study[8] classified the attitudes of labour unions towards technological change into five categories:[9]

1. *encouragement* – when the union urges the employer to adopt new methods to increase productivity in order to stay competitive.
2. *willing acceptance* – when the union does not oppose the introduction of technological innovation.
3. *adjustment* – when the union accepts the changes and focuses on collective bargaining to cushion its members from any negative effects of the change.
4. *competition* – when the members increase productivity through more efficient use of old methods; for example seeking to retain the traditional methods of operation by accepting wage cuts and/or agreeing to the elimination of certain work rules.
5. *opposition* – when the union conducts one or several work stoppages over the changes or flatly refuses to allow its members to use the new technology.

The study found that 48.9 per cent of unions indicated *willing acceptance* of technological changes, 24.5 per cent demonstrated opposition, 23.9 per cent indicated adjustment, 2.7 per cent demonstrated *encouragement*, and 0 per cent indicated competition.[10] In relation to those who indicated opposition, the study emphasises that such was *the initial* reaction to the new technology, and that it was usually followed by either willing acceptance or adjustment.[11]

Generally, the attitudes of unions are a reflection of the employment records of the industries in their jurisdictions: *positive attitudes* can be expected to exist in industries which have recorded expanding employment, even though significant technological changes may have taken place in them; the attitudes will be *negative* in industries which experienced declining employment, even though technological changes in them may have been sporadic and minimal; and an attitude of *indifference* may prevail amongst unions whose members have not been effected by technological or any other changes. In addition, attitudes may be effected by perceived management attitudes towards the employees: where management attitudes are perceived to be understanding and reasonable, union attitudes may be generally consenting; where management attitudes are perceived to be indifferent or non-committal, union attitudes will be conditional and protective.

The majority of union leaders neither oppose outright nor advocate technological changes. Instead, they declare *conditional acceptance*, and then seek to negotiate the conditions under which they will not oppose their introduction. Amongst the specific union conditions put on the table in recent years, *job protection* has been given the highest priority. This has been particularly the case in instances where major skills were affected adversely, and where alternative employment opportunities in local and regional markets were limited. Job protection involves, of course, the negotiation of not only a guarantee of employment for the displaced workers, but also management commitments regarding training and retraining, transfers, the nature of employment activities in alternative positions, wage guarantees, and related issues. Where the nature of new technology and production processes preclude the possibility of retraining and reemployment, the accommodative arrangements involve placement with other firms, severance pay, early retirement, income maintenance plans, and supplementary unemployment benefits.

An examination of collective agreements will reveal a wide gap between what unions have wanted and what they have achieved. Although many companies have introduced a variety of accommodative arrangements, particularly for long service employees, many such arrangements have been largely ad hoc and at management's discretion.

Two explanations can be offered for the limited accommodative provisions in collective agreements: one is, the continuing resistance of management to discussions on the issue of technological change and its employment implications. Technological change continues to be regarded a management prerogative, to be exercised at will as part of management's right to manage. The employment implications are taken to be a natural consequence, with necessary manpower adjustments and accommodations to be introduced at management's initiative, on an ad hoc basis, with or without negotiation with worker representatives. The second explanation for the limited contractual provisions is the unions' *reactive* approach to bargaining: where technological changes have been significant, and adverse effects have caused agitation amongst workers, unions have reacted forcefully and have insisted on the negotiation of appropriate contractual provisions; where changes have had limited adverse effects on workers, and generally satisfactory accommodations have been implemented, the issues have not become subject to negotiation; and where no technological changes of consequence have been implemented, the issue has not arisen. Had the approach to bargaining been *anticipatory, instead of reactive,* the evidence undoubtedly would have been different. But, account must be taken of two realities of the negotiating process: one is the reality that it is difficult to get workers out on strike on anticipated possibilities; and the other reality is the give and take of the bargaining process. It is a realistic possibility that unions have traded-off negative technological effects for issues on which they put higher priority, such as wages, hours of work and pensions.

It is in the nature of labour-management relations to deal with current and critical issues, and leave potential problems for the future, when they become critical. For example, even though it is widely known that micro-electronic technology will impact severely on employment in service activities, most public service unions have given no indication of intent to make the issue of technology and its employment effects a priority item in the negotiating agenda. This tendency to await until developments reach a critical phase before they are brought to the bargaining table contributes to the crisis environment in which negotiations are carried out. A crisis environment dictates speedy solutions; and speedy solutions are oftentimes not necessarily long-lasting solutions.

The absence of contractual provisions does not mean, of course, that accommodative arrangements do not in fact exist. It means only that they are not specifically provided in collective agreements. This is in accord with the prevailing attitude of management that technological changes are a managerial prerogative, and accommodative arrangements related to such changes should remain ad hoc and discretionary with management. Sporadic information suggests the existence of widespread ad hoc arrangements, largely negotiated outside the provisions of the collective agreements in force. The question remains whether the matter can be left to ad hoc arrangements. The anticipated acceleration in the rate of technological change seems to dictate a formalisation in adjustment processes.

Satisfactory accommodations on an ad hoc basis are possible only as long as the technological changes are minor, and effects on workers are minimal. When the rate of technological change accelerates, affecting adversely increasing numbers of workers, the ad hoc, management initiated, approach to accommodation will not be viable. This suggests the need for changes in approaches to the formulation and implementation of accommodative arrangements. If the bargaining process does not evolve satisfactory standing procedures, the legislative process will have to set general guidelines.

The general policy of North American unions has been to focus on the accommodative aspects of technological changes – the negotiation of terms and conditions on behalf of workers who are adversely affected by technological changes. Implicit in such a policy is acceptance of all technological changes as necessary, and recognition of management's right to conceive, design and implement changes without consultation with unions, regardless of the nature and magnitude of effects the changes may have on the employment and welfare of workers. Yet it is generally recognised that most decisions are selected from amongst alternative possibilities. Different choices often entail different effects and different costs – different technological systems, implemented at different times, over different periods of time, will often have different effects. In view of this, it is to be expected that workers would not be satisfied with policy approaches that seek to accommodate effects which are presented as if dictated by the technology with no possible alternatives. While it may be true that alternatives to established systems are possibly limited, it is not necessarily true that they are equally limited at the planning and design phases. Inevitably, when a system is in place, discussion must focus on accommodations; but, when a system is at the planning and designing phases, discussions can focus on alternative systems and approaches to implementation which will minimise the adverse effects on employees. It is a reflection on the state of labour-management relations, and on management's perception of its responsibility towards non-management employees, when management plans, designs and implements changes without consultation with representatives of the employees.[12] At the time when management begins to share information with representatives of employees during the planning stages, and consults with them throughout the period of planning, design and implementation, labour–management relations will be said to be in a state of mutual trust, confidence and respect. When the labour–management environment is characterised as adversarial, which precludes the possibility of consultation, cooperation and mutuality, adverse effects on employees and employment will be resolved through negotiated rules and regulations or through the legislative process. Implicit in this historical reality is a lesson and a warning which the parties do not appear to have recognised, namely, failure to find satisfactory solutions to problems arising from change through negotiations constitutes an open invitation to the legislative process to intervene and set general rules and regulations for all. Each time the legislative process establishes a new set of rules and regulations, the collective bargaining process suffers another bit of erosion in its foundation and scope. Therefore, if free collective bargaining is important to labour and management, it is incumbent on them to avoid giving the legislative process justifications for intervention. The anticipated acceleration in the rate of technological changes over the next two decades will severely test the resolve of labour and management to preserve the institution of collective bargaining.

CONFLICT AND RESOLUTION THROUGH BARGAINING

Labour-management conflicts on the issue of technological change are derived from a fundamental difference of opinion on the relationship between "men and machines". Employees and their spokesmen have generally taken the stand that technological changes should be viewed as *complimentary* to workers, benefiting both the workers and their employers; whereas management has tended to view technological changes as *substitutes* for labour. Employee organisations have sought to protect their members against displacement and to obtain a share of the benefits generated by technological changes; whereas management has sought to ensure that the investment in technological changes becomes manifested in higher productivity and profits.

Few conflicts have centered on the issue of whether a technological change should be put into effect: the issues of conflict have related largely to what should be done to offset the adverse effects on employees, on terms and conditions of employment, and on recognised work rules and practices. It is the inability to agree upon satisfactory accommodative arrangements on these issues that has led to conflicts, not the technological changes themselves.

An examination of some major conflicts in construction, printing, the railways and the docks that related to the issue of technological change will reveal two main obstacles to the finding of mutually satisfactory accommodative arrangements: the concept of managerial prerogatives is one, and the other is the linkage of accommodative arrangements to other terms and conditions of employment in the negotiation of collective agreements. Generally, management has regarded technological changes, including organisational and operational changes and changes in products, as non-negotiable issues falling within the domain of management rights. Labour's response has been that although decisions on technological changes are a managerial prerogative, their effects on employees and on the terms and conditions of their employment are negotiable issues.

THE ROLE OF GOVERNMENT

Satisfactory relations between labour and management will not evolve in an environment of legal restraints. It is preferable that the parties themselves impose restraints on themselves by mutual agreement. Therefore, the aim of legislation should be to facilitate the removal of obstacles to mutually agreed upon restraints and to the establishment by the parties of effective dispute–settlement machinery. Restraining legislation should be limited to those aspects of labour–management relations which facilitate collective bargaining and protect the public interest – recognition by employers of certified employee organisations for bargaining purposes, bargaining in good faith, and prohibition of activities by either or both parties that are deemed to be detrimental to the public. When issues arise which one of the parties considers vital for its growth and strength, whereas the other refuses to negotiate on them, compulsory arbitration becomes the only just and expeditious mechanism: a party which refuses to negotiate cannot be caused to negotiate; it can be compelled to make a proposal or counter-proposal, but cannot be made to engage in the game of give-and-take, which is the meaning of negotiation.

Account must be taken also of the possibility that the parties will enter into agreements that are beneficial to themselves, but detrimental to the communities in which they are located or to the public at large. This dictates a role for government: when proposed technological changes indicate significant effects on communities or on the public at large, the public interest dictates government involvement to ensure suitable accommodative arrangements. Negotiations between the employer and employee organisations will necessarily be limited to issues that relate to adversely affected employees; negotiations must take place between the enterprise and government on issues that relate to adverse effects on communities and the public at large.

It is recognised that from the standpoint of industrial efficiency and economic progress, technological, organisational and operational changes must remain a managerial prerogative; but it should also be recognised that the implementation of changes which have adverse and dislocative effects on workers and communities must be made conditional on satisfactory offsetting and accommodative arrangements with both the employees and the communities affected.

Technological, operational and organisational changes are not conceived, formulated, produced and implemented overnight; they are conceived, discussed, researched, designed, tested, discussed again, produced and then implemented. Therefore, it cannot be argued that there is no time to discuss with representatives of employee organisations the implications for employment security, skills, wage differentials, employment classifications, relocations and other. Indeed, it should be mandatory that enterprises and employee organisations undertake studies jointly to determine precisely the potential effects on employees and employment. The findings of such studies should provide the basis for discussions and negotiations. Too often negotiations are carried out in an atmosphere of uncertainty on the nature and extent of adverse effects, which becomes in itself a source of irritation and conflict. Furthermore, negotiations on accommodative arrangements are frequently carried out in conjunction with negotiations for the standard contract on terms and conditions of employment, which is not a desirable practice. The effects of any given technological, operational or organisational change are identifiable and measurable: negotiations on accommodative arrangements should relate to those effects only. Attempts to link such accommodative arrangements to general terms and conditions of employment negotiated in the standard contract, have frequently resulted in the prolongation of negotiations, delays in implementation of change, and occasionally in conflict. Technological change is too important to economic development and growth for it or its effects to be traded-off against other terms and conditions of employment. Its implementation and accommodations related to it, should be negotiated and arbitrated outside the regular employment contract.

TECHNOLOGICAL CHANGES, WORK RULES AND EMPLOYMENT PRACTICES

The effects of technological, operational and organisational changes on work rules, occupational jurisdictions and employment practices have caused more conflicts between management and employee organisations than any other effects on terms and conditions of employment. Even reductions in employment have been accepted and accommodated more readily than potential threats to the work activities performed by individual occupations.

This issue will become increasingly critical as microelectronic instruments and processes encroach on work functions and make possible their performance with less knowledge than the knowledge of those who now perform the work functions. The response of individual occupations to the encroachment on their traditional jurisdictions will depend largely on the ways in which individual members of the occupations perceive their work functions relative to the work functions performed by members of related occupational categories: the more cooperative the relationship in the performance of work activities, the lesser is likely to be the confrontation; conversely, the lower the esteem one occupation has of another, the greater the possibility of conflict when changes in technology dictate cooperation and the downward transfer of work functions.

Some occupations and organisations are, of course, more notorious than others in the imposition of work rules and employment practices designed to protect practitioners of their occupations against potential interlopers whether they be human, material or organisational. The most notorious are the legalised professional monopolies of lawyers, physicians, and dentists, followed by printers, electricians, musicians, plumbers, bricklayers, painters and so on. The degree of notoriety is measured in terms of the amount of unnecessary work they do, and insist that it be done; and the extent to which they prohibit or make it very difficult for anyone other than a certified member of their occupation to perform any functions designated as being within the competence of the occupation.[13]

It should be recognised that all work rules and employment practices imposed by employee organisations and occupational associations are not necessarily irrational acts of irresponsible individuals. Workers need protection against unreasonable work expectations of employers, and consumers must be protected from unqualified individuals offering specialised services. The determination of how many workers should be required in a given setting for the production of a given quantity of goods or for the performance of a given range of functions, how long they should work without interruption, what kinds of knowledge and skill they should have, and what should be expected of them given that knowledge and skill, are not issues that should be decided unilaterally be either party. These are issues for employer–employee consultative committees at the shop and office level.

As indicated at the beginning of this section, management have tended to regard improvements in technology and operations as possible partial or full substitutes for labour; whereas employees and their organisations have tended to regard them as compliments. The leader of an employee organisation expressed the employee's stand on the matter in the following way:

> When improvements in technology and operations cause the elimination of some work-functions formerly performed by our members we regard this to be a change favouring the workers. Over a long period of time technological improvements were regarded from the standpoint of the benefits that would accrue to the companies only. We regarded this to be wrong. Now we are determined to make certain that the benefits accrue to the workers as well. It appears inconsistent to us that a technological improvement which reduces the amount of labour necessary for the performance of certain functions should not be reflected in the work-loads of the workers themselves. Yet, when we insist on this, we are accused of imposing so-called featherbedding rules.[14]

In response, management spokesmen argue that workers do benefit from the increases in productivity generated by technological and operational improvements, and that they will benefit even more if redundant workers were to be released from employment. Neither the enterprise nor the employees benefit from the retention of workers whose services are no longer required.

The latter is based on the premise that the amount of work, worktime and work-effort that a worker or a group of workers must offer are established scientifically, and that, therefore, any technological and operational changes that would cause a process of production to require less work-effort and generally less labour must necessarily result in a reduction of the labour force. There is no such scientific or natural law: the work-effort required has been largely established by the nature of production processes; and work-time is established in negotiations.[15] Both have changed dramatically over the years, which in itself is evidence that they are subject to change.

This does not mean, of course, that technological and operational changes do not or should not have labour displacing effects, or that work-rules and employment practices should not be adjusted to accommodate new processes of production and new capital–labour relationships. What they do mean is that accommodative changes in work-rules and employment practices should be formulated through negotiation, and suitable provisions should be made for the re-training, relocation and re-employment of those who will be displaced.

The existence of occupational regulations regarding who can do what, where, when and how much will continue to cause conflicts between labour and management. Inevitably, such regulations prevent some people from doing what they would like to do, prevent others from working wherever they would like to work, some are prevented from doing things the way they would like to do them, and others are prevented from working as long as they would like to work, as fast as they would like, and as much as they are able to produce.

It is a peculiarity of our social structure and social values to associate such regulations with the unions of wage-earners and to condemn them as "restrictive work rules" which cause output to be limited and costs to be increased. Yet, the regulations under which professional workers work are far more restrictive

than any regulations to be found in labour–management contracts. For example, the legal profession has such an absolute
control of the judicial system as to make it virtually impossible
for anyone not a member of the profession to function within it.
Indeed, the profession has succeeded in legalising relationships
amongst individuals, groups and institutions to such an extent as
to make it inadvisable for anyone to enter into any relationship
without formal contractual documentation executed by a member of the profession.

The primary reason for occupational rules and regulations is
to restrict competition from substitute occupations, instruments,
processes and products. The primary motivation is to provide a
measure of employment security in the case of occupations
which feel insecure, and to ensure relatively high incomes in the
case of occupations which have been given legislative monopoly
powers. Musicians fall within the first category, physicians and
lawyers within the second.[16]

An example of the first is provided in the 1974 agreement
between the International Typographical Union and the New
York Times and The Daily News: it is a seven year agreement
under which the eighteen hundred workers covered are guaranteed lifetime employment and/or income security, and the two
newspapers are free to introduce any kind of technological
changes – computers and electronic typesetting equipment – and
to determine their manpower needs.[17] The decision of the employees to enter into such an agreement demonstrates that in
their case the underlying reason for occupational rules and
regulations was insecurity of employment. The guarantee of
employment removed the need for measures designed to provide
a measure of employment security. Given similar guarantees to
similarly placed occupations would undoubtedly result in similar responses: there would be no need for "restrictive" rules and
regulations.

Such a response cannot be expected from the second group,
since their motivation is the earning of monopoly income. The
only way in which restrictive work rules and regulations can be
removed from the work processes in which physicians, lawyers,
dentists and such other occupations function is to take away
from them the control of production processes in which they are
engaged and to remove the legislative monopoly powers given to
their organisations. Unless this is done, neither their incomes

nor the costs of institutions in which they render their services can be controlled. An examination of labour-management conflicts commonly attributed to technological changes will establish that most such conflicts were not so much the result of the technological changes as such, as they were the result of failures to consult in advance of implementation, and failure to make adequate accommodative arrangements for adversely affected workers – for their re-employment, re-training, relocation and other. The fundamental problem appears to be a tendency on the part of management to plan in detail every aspect of technological and operational changes, except the human aspect. All pronouncements on the implications for employees, for the affected communities and for society at large appear as an afterthought – as if it were a law of nature, an imperative, over which management has no control, and by implication, no responsibility. The explanation for this will be found in the management ethic which views the negative effects of technological change as the price to be paid, the cost to be borne by society, for economic progress. The onus is clearly on society to decide whether it is to its net benefit to tolerate such an ethic. Alternative approaches do exist; and in their existence originate the conflicts.

SUMMARY AND CONCLUSION: THREE MYTHS

Three myths have been identified in relation to technology and collective bargaining: one myth is that technology is deterministic in its effects on the organisation of work, on employment, occupations and conditions of work; the second myth is that collective bargaining has been and is the best mechanism for dealing with the effects of technological changes on employment and occupations; and the third myth is that efficiency considerations are responsible for management resistance to consultative arrangements with labour on matters that relate to technological changes and their effects on employees and employment. All of these will become the most critical issues of the 1990s.

The first myth concerns the issue of the extent to which effects attributed to technology are in fact determined by technology, and the extent to which they are determined by human decisions. Much has been written on the effects of technology, alleging implicitly or explicitly that they are dictated by technology, and that the resultant costs on society are the costs of technological progress. The impression has been created that any rules and regulations that would require the reduction of adverse effects would impair technological progress. Yet, an examination of the evidence suggests that the effects of individual technologies have varied significantly amongst processes in different industries, regions and countries, which suggests in turn that it is not the technologies that have dictated the outcomes, but rather human decisions. Most often differences in negative effects appear to be the result of (1) inadequate or imperfect knowledge in the application of technologies; (2) imperfections in the technologies themselves, which often are the result of inadequate testing prior to implementation; (3) inadequate effort to determine the effects on activities and processes removed from the production process; (4) changes in the organisation of work to accommodate the technology with little regard to other implications; and (5) haste in implementation motivated by competition and cost considerations.

It is important to note in relation to the last of these that it is not total costs that are considered; the consideration is limited to direct production costs. The ability of enterprises to transfer potential technology-related costs from themselves to employees and society at large hides the real costs of technological change and gives thereby a comparative advantage to technology over labour in production processes. The question arises where would be the advantage if technology were to bear all the costs associated with its operation.

The second myth concerns the appropriateness of the collective bargaining process for the introduction of satisfactory accommodative responses to technological changes. The evidence for this is contained in technology-related provisions of collective agreements, and the effectiveness with which existing provisions have been executed. The conclusion in relation to both is that they have been very limited: limited provisions and limited effectiveness.

It can be argued, of course, that the problems heretofore have not been so widespread and serious to warrant priority consideration in bargaining agendas. Now that microelectronic technology has elevated the potential problems to the level of actual problems, appropriate priority will be assigned and the outcomes will be different.

Notwithstanding the evidence of some such moves by labour organisations, and some collective agreements that indicate desirable outcomes, progress to-date has been very limited. Furthermore, microelectronic technology dictates *a comprehensive overall approach to its employment effects*, not an approach that is limited to the employment functions of individual workers or to employment in individual firms, or industries. It was noted that unlike electromechanical instruments and processes whose effects on employment and skills are for the most part limited to the point or place of application, the effects of microelectronic technology can be widespread. The technology is pervasive in application, and the convergence of computers and telecommunications systems into telematic networks implies nationwide and worldwide effects by the simple act of establishing a link to an established network. This new reality suggests a different approach to bargaining, perhaps a multi-union, multi-industry approach.

It suggests also a need for consultation and cooperation amongst unions *in their approaches* to negotiation on technological issues, and coordination in responses to the challenges of emerging microelectronic processes. The pervasiveness of the technology and the highly diffusive effects of telematic networks, dictate a more active role for coordinating bodies of employee organisations. The alternative to coordination is probably amalgamation of employment-related organisations.

The structure of collective bargaining in North America and Great Britain is too decentralised to be effective in the setting of general standards. Throughout the history of labour organisation and collective bargaining, whenever general standards became a desirable social goal, they were established by the legislative process. As long as changes in technology and accommodations to it remain sporadic there will be no pressure on the legislative process to act. This is not dissimilar to the failure of the legislative process to become involved in the early conflicts between labour and management over organisational activities and efforts to engage in collective bargaining. But, when such activities became widespread, and it became necessary to set general standards, the legislative process stepped in. The same can be expected in relation to technology-related accommodative arrangements.

The role of collective bargaining in this is the same as what it has been throughout history on matters of general economic and social interest, namely, to set the standards for the legislative process. This is a critical role. In the absence of such guidance the legislative process could well introduce standards that are unacceptable to either or both parties. Therefore, if the leading players in the labour–management arena wish to influence the standards that will ultimately emerge, it would be well that they take the matter seriously and begin to consider the nature of accommodations that are compatible with criteria of efficiency and equity to enterprises and workers alike.

The third myth is that efficiency considerations motivate management in its resistance to the establishment of consultative processes with labour for the discussion of matters that relate to technological change and its effects on employees and employment. Management has generally taken the position that its responsibility to manage the enterprise efficiently will be impaired if it did not have unilateral power to make decisions.

Two fundamental questions relate to the issue of management prerogatives: one is, how much unilateral decision-making power does management need for the efficient management of enterprises; and the other is, to what extent will managerial effectiveness in the management function be impaired if discussions with employee representatives were to precede decisions on matters that effect the employment of employees. The history of management practice provides evidence of significant changes in methods and scope of management over time, involving considerable sharing of powers. There is no evidence of impairment in efficiency as a direct result of changes in decision-making within the management structure, nor is there evidence of impairment in efficiency as a result of the system of collective determination of some of the terms and conditions of employment. In the absence of evidence that the efficiency of enterprises is impaired by consultations and collective decision-making, the insistence that the omnipotent authority of management be safeguarded is based on considerations of managerial power, not on the consideration of the interests of the enterprise.

Notes and References

INTRODUCTION

1. An address to a conference on "Labour Relations in the 1980s", organized by the Personnel Association of Toronto, on 23 June 1980, reported in *Collective Bargaining, Arbitration* (CCH Canadian Ltd, 15 Oct. 1980) pp. 6507–11.

CHAPTER 1 THE COLLECTIVE BARGAINING PROCESS

1. Daniel J. B. Mitchell, *Unions, Wages and Inflation* (Washington, D.C.: The Brookings Institution, 1980). There prevails a general view that European employers do not regard employee organizations as negatively as North American Employers do. See: Everett M. Kassalow, "Industrial Conflict and Consensus in the United States and Western Europe: a Comparative Analysis", in Industrial Relations Research Association, *Proceedings of the Thirtieth Annual Winter Meeting* (Madison, Wisconsin: 1978).
2. Clark Kerr, *et al.* state: "A primary concern of management, in its relationship to workers, is to establish, to make legitimate, and to maintain its authority", *Industrialism and Industrial Man* (New York: Oxford University Press, 1964) p. 125.
3. D. Quinn Mills, "Reforming the U.S. System of Collective Bargaining", *The Monthly Labor Review*, 106 (Mar. 1983) pp. 18–22.
4. Sumner H. Slichter, J. J. Healy, and E. R. Livernash, *The Impact of Collective Bargaining on Management* (Washington, D.C.: The Brookings Institution, 1960).
5. Walter Y. Oi considers this issue in "Labor as a Quasi-Fixed Factor", *Journal of Political Economy*, LXX (Dec. 1962) pp. 538–55.
6. A good historical perspective on the evolution of employee organization in the United States and Great Britain (where it all started) can be gained from the following sources: For Britain: E. H. Phelps Brown, *The Growth of British Industrial Relations* (London: Macmillan, 1959); and Askwith, Sir George Rankin, *Industrial Problems and Disputes* (London: John Murray, 1920). For the United States: R. F. Hoxie, *Trade Unionism in the United States* (New York: D. Appleton-Century-Crofts, 1924); and H. A. Mills and R. E. Montgomery, *Organized Labor* (New York: McGraw-Hill, 1945).

159

7. Clark Kerr, "Collective Bargaining in Crises?", *Saturday Review* (13 Jan., 1962) p. 20.
8. Sir Otto Kahn-Freund, *Labour Relations: Heritage and Adjustment* (Oxford University Press, 1979) p. 22.
9. Constraints on this are more likely from sources external to the firm such as Equal Employment Opportunity Acts, Human Rights Legislation, the Certification of Skills, and closed shop arrangements which would dictate that management hire only union members.
10. S. H. Slichter, *et al.*, ibid., pp. 947–51.
11. Lloyd Ulman (ed.), *Challenges to Collective Bargaining*, (Englewood Cliffs, N.J.: Prentice-Hall Inc., 1967) p. 1.
12. W. L. Mackenzie King, *Industry and Humanity* (Cambridge, Mass.: Houghton Mifflin Company, The University Press, 1918) p. 518.

CHAPTER 2 POWER SHARING: PROTECTION OF SELF-INTEREST

1. Herbert A. Simon, "What is Industrial Democracy?", *Challenge*, 25 (Jan./Feb. 1983) pp. 30–9.
2. Clark Kerr and his associates discuss different management responses to pressures from workers to share their authority in *Industrialism and Industrial Man*, pp. 128–32.
3. Charles D. King and Mark van de Vall, *Models of Industrial Democracy: Consultation, Co-determination and Workers' Management* (The Hague: Mouton Publishers, 1978).
4. Herbert A. Simon, ibid., pp. 36–7.
5. Charles D. King and Mark van de Vall, ibid.
6. This impression is attested by observations of US unionists who visited Sweden in 1981. See: Eric Einhorn and John Logue, "Can American Trade Unions Learn from the Swedish Shop Floor?: a Round-table Discussion", *Working Life in Sweden* (A publication of the Swedish Information Office in New York, no. 2, Mar. 1982). Also see, Douglas Soutar, "Co-Determination, Industrial Democracy and The Role of Management", in Industrial Relations Research Association, *Proceedings of the Twenty-Sixth Annual Winter Meeting* (New York: 28–9 Dec. 1973) pp. 1–7.
7. Eric Einhorn and John Logue, ibid., p. 10.
8. Ibid., p. 11.
9. Charles D. King and Mark van de Vall, ibid., pp. 101–2 and pp. 192–4.
10. Robert J. Flannagan, "The National Accord as a Social Contract", *Industrial and Labor Relations Review*, XXIV (Oct. 1980) pp. 35–50.
11. Soutar, ibid., p. 3.
12. Soutar, ibid., p. 3.
13. Robert J. Kuhne, *Co-Determination in Business: Workers' Representatives in the Boardroom* (New York: Preager Publishers, 1980).
14. Hans Seidel, "Incomes Policy in Austria", *Challenge*, XXIV (Sept./Oct. 1981) p. 58.
15. Instructive discussion on this issue will be found in Robert J. Kuhne, ibid.;

James Furlong, *Labor in the Boardroom*, (1977); and Alfred L. Trimm, *The False Promise of Co-determination*, (1980).

16. Sir Otto Kahn-Freund, ibid., p. 3.
17. Sir Otto Kahn-Freund, ibid., p. 19.
18. Sir Otto Kahn-Freund, ibid., pp. 1–31.
19. Sir Otto Kahn-Freund, ibid., p. 43.
20. Stephen Hill examines this issue in relation to the 'shop floor' in *Competition and Control at Work: The New Industrial Sociology* (Cambridge, Mass.: MIT Press, 1981).

CHAPTER 3   THE STRUCTURE OF COLLECTIVE BARGAINING

1. John T. Dunlop, "Structure of Collective Bargaining", in Industrial Relations Research Association, *The Next Twenty-Five Years of Industrial Relations* (Madison, Wisc.: 1973) p. 10.
2. Daniel Quinn Mills, *Labor–Management Relations* (New York: McGraw-Hill, 1978) p. 404.
3. S. M. Jamieson, *Industrial Conflict in Canada* (Economic Council of Canada, Discussion Paper no. 142, Dec. 1979) p. 1.
4. Arnold Weber, "Stability and Change in the Structure of Collective Bargaining", in Lloyd Ulman (ed.), *Challenges to Collective Bargaining* (Englewood Cliffs, N.J.: Prentice-Hall, 1967) pp. 30–2.
5. Canada, Task Force on Labour Relations, *Canadian Industrial Relations* (The Queen's Printer, Ottawa, 1969) p. 164.
6. Ibid., p. 165.
7. Herbert R. Northrop, "Reflections on Bargaining Structure Change", in Industrial Relations Research Association, *Proceedings of the Twenty-Sixth Annual Winter Meeting* (New York: 28–9 Dec. 1973) p. 137.
8. Gideon Chitayat, *Trade Union Mergers and Labor Conglomerates* (New York: Praeger, 1979).
9. This has been found to be the case in the United States. See: Arnold R. Weber, "Stability and Change in the Structure of Collective Bargaining", in Lloyd Ulman (ed.), *Challenges to Collective Bargaining* (Prentice-Hall, 1967) pp. 13–36; and J. T. Dunlop, ibid., p. 13.
10. H. S. Slichter *et al.*, ibid., pp. 918–45.
11. A study of nine Western Countries, including the United States, determined that there has been an increasing concentration in the structure of unionism and collective bargaining. John P. Windmiller, "Concentration Trends in Union Structure: an International Comparison", *Industrial and Labor Relations Review* XXXV (Oct. 1981) pp. 43–57. The trends towards concentration in the US have been in evidence for some time. See: Philip Taft, "Internal Union Structure and Functions", in Industrial Relations Research Association, *The Next Twenty-Five Years of Industrial Relations* Madison, Wisc.: 1973) pp. 1–9.
12. S. H. Slichter, *et al.*, ibid., pp. 14–5. The authors state: "Employers as a rule prefer longer contract terms than do unions since the experience of

most employers has been that every time a contract is renewed, the employer has to make more concessions." ibid., p. 15.

13. W. E. Simkin, "Refusals to Ratify Contracts", *Industrial and Labor Relations Review*, 21 (July 1968) pp. 518–40.

14. Donald R. Burke and Lester Rubin, "Is Contract Rejection a Major Collective Bargaining Problem?", *Industrial and Labor Relations Review*, 26 (Jan. 1973) pp. 820–33.

CHAPTER 4   THE WAGE AND SALARY STRUCTURE

1. US Department of Labour, Bureau of Labor Statistics, *Monthly Labor Review*, 107 (Jan. 1984) Table 12, p. 96.

2. *Fortune* (12 July 1982) pp. 42-52.

3. This issue is examined in considerable detail by Lester C. Thurow in *Generating Inequality: Mechanisms of Distribution in the U.S. Economy* (New York: Basic Books, 1975); and in *The Zero-Sum Society: Distribution and Possibilities for Economic Change* (New York: Basic Books, 1980).

4. Dan Usher discusses this issue and its implications for income policies in *The Economic Prerequisite for Democracy* (London: Basil Blackwell, 1981).

5. H. Wallich and S. Weintraub have proposed such a policy as an anti-inflationary measure, in "A Tax-Based Incomes Policy", *Journal of Economic Issues*, 5 (June 1971) pp. 1–19.

6. A very creditable examination of this issue will be found in Lester C. Thurow, *Generating Inequality . . .*, (1975).

7. Ibid., p. 22.

8. This matter is discussed by John Rawls, *A Theory of Justice* (Cambridge, Mass.: Harvard University Press, 1971); Lester Thurow, *Generating Inequality . . .*, (1975), and *The Zero-Sum Society . . .*, (1980); Dan Usher, *The Economic Prerequisite for Democracy*, (1981); and George Gilder, *Wealth and Poverty* (New York: Basic Books, 1981).

9. More so in Europe and Britain than in North America. The British in particular have demonstrated a very high propensity to enquire into the level and distribution of incomes. More has been written in Britain about income policies than in any other country. In the past two decades (1962–82) thirteen white papers on income policies and issues related to incomes have been issued. In addition, the National Board for Prices and Incomes issued scores of reports on pay and productivity which contain pronouncements on income policy.

10. For the US, see Harry Ober, "Occupational Wage Differentials, 1907–1947", *Monthly Labor Review*, LXVII (Aug. 1948) pp. 127–34; for the UK: E. H. Phelps Brown, *A Century of Pay* (London: Macmillan, 1968). See also M. W. Reder, "The Theory of Occupational Wage Differentials", *American Economic Review*, XLV (Dec. 1955) pp. 833–52.

11. Adam Smith, *The Wealth of Nations* (Chicago: Richard D. Irwin, 1963) pp. 79–84.

12. This issue is discussed in detail by Lester C. Thurow in *The Zero-Sum Society . . .*, (1980).

13. M. W. Reder, ibid.; and Gary S. Becker, *Human Capital: a Theoretical and Empirical Analysis, with Special Reference to Education* (New York: National Bureau of Economic Research, 1964).
14. A. W. Phillips, "The Relation Between Unemployment and the Rate of Change in Money Wage Rates in the United Kingdom, 1861–1957", *Economica*, 25 (Nov. 1958) pp. 285–99.
15. Reference is made to the telephone industry, but the communication is unsigned and undated.
16. N. Kaldor, "Alternative Theories of Distribution", *The Review of Economic Studies*, XXIII (1955) pp. 83–100; and C. Kerr, "Labor's Share and the Labor Movement", in G. W. Taylor and F. C. Pierson (eds), *New Concepts in Wage Determination* (New York: McGraw-Hill, 1957).
17. This is the conclusion that can be drawn from the University of Michigan's surveys on quality of work life. See the sequence of surveys conducted since 1969, *Quality of Work Life* (Institute for Social Research, University of Michigan, 1969, 1973, 1977).
18. The work to which most frequent reference is made in relation to needs and goals in A. H. Maslow's hierarchy of needs. See A. H. Maslow, *Motivation and Personality* (New York: Harper & Row, 1954).
19. Michael Schuster, "The Impact of Union-Management Co-operation on Productivity and Employment", *Industrial and Labor Relations Review*, XXXVI (Apr. 1983) pp. 415–30.
20. An excellent wide-ranging article on this subject: Thomas E. Weisskopf, Samuel Bowles, and David M. Gordon, "Hearts and Minds: A Social Model of U.S. Productivity Growth", *Brookings Papers on Economic Activity*, II (1983) pp. 381–450.

CHAPTER 5   PATTERNS OF WAGE BARGAINING AND WAGE REGULATIONS

1. For a discussion on this issue see: John T. Dunlop, "Working Toward Consensus", an Interview in *Challenge* 25 (July/Aug. 1982) pp. 26–34; Audrey Freedman, "A Fundamental Change in Wage Bargaining", *Challenge*, 25 (July/Aug. 1982) pp. 14–7; Audrey Freedman and William E. Fulmer, "Last Rites for Pattern Bargaining", *Harvard Business Review*, 60 (Mar./Apr. 1982) pp. 30–48; and Daniel J. B. Mitchell, "Recent Union Contract Concessions", *Brookings Papers on Economic Activity*, 1 (1982) pp. 165–204.
2. Audrey Freedman, ibid.
3. Daniel J. B. Mitchell, "Recent Union Contract Concessions", *Brookings Papers on Economic Activity*, I (1982) pp. 165–204; and Peter Henle, "Reverse Collective Bargaining?: a Look at Some Union Concession Situations", *Industrial and Labor Relations Review*, XXVI (Apr. 1973) pp. 956–68.
4. Robert E. Hall, "The Importance of Lifetime Jobs in the U.S. Economy", *American Economic Review*, LXXII (Sept. 1982) pp. 716–24.
5. It is important to note, however, that in Japan payments to labour are in two parts – the wage and an annual or semi-annual bonus which is based

on profits. The bonus tends to vary with variations in activity, which may be interpreted to constitute a cost of employment security.

6. Daniel J. B. Mitchell, "Gain-sharing: an Anti-Inflation Reform", *Challenge*, 25 (July/Aug. 1982) pp. 18–25.
7. Daniel J. B. Mitchell, ibid., p. 24.
8. Robert J. Flannagan, David W. Soskice, and Lloyd Ulman, *Unionism, Economic Stabilization and Incomes Policy: European Experience* (Washington: The Brookings Institution, 1983); and Hugh A. Clegg, *The Changing System of Industrial Relations in Great Britain* (Oxford: Basil Blackwell, 1979) pp. 345–82.
9. John T. Dunlop, "The Task of Contemporary Wage Theory", in George W. Taylor and Frank C. Pierson (eds), *New Concepts in Wage Determination* (New York: McGraw-Hill, 1957); Clark Kerr, "Wage Relationships – The Comparative Impact of Market and Power Forces", in John T. Dunlop (ed.), *The Theory of Wage Determination*, (London: Macmillan, 1957); and M. Levinson, "Pattern Bargaining: a Case Study of the Automobile Workers", *Quarterly Journal of Economics*, LXXIV (May 1960) pp. 296–317.
10. Lloyd Ulman, (ed.), *Collective Bargaining and Government Policies* (OECD, Paris 1979).
11. Robert E. Hall, "Employment Fluctuations and Wage Rigidity", *Brookings Papers on Economic Activity*, I (1980) pp. 91–123, plus "Comments", pp. 124–41.
12. A good examination of the role and outcomes of arbitration will be found in Peter Feuille, "Selected Benefits and Costs of Compulsory Arbitration", *Industrial and Labor Relations Review*, XXXIII (Oct. 1979) pp. 64–76.
13. Milton Derber and Martin Wagner, "Public Sector Bargaining and Budget Making Under Fiscal Adversity", *Industrial and Labor Relations Review*, XXXIII (Oct. 1979) pp. 18–23.
14. The standard Keynesian posture. See: John Maynard Keynes, *The General Theory of Employment, Interest and Money* (London: Macmillan, 1936).
15. K. Brunner and A. Meltzer (eds), *The Economics of Wage and Price Controls* (New York: North-Holland, 1976); C. Goodwin (ed.), *Extortion and Controls: the Search for a Wage-Price Policy, 1945–1971* (Washington: The Brookings Institution, 1975); and Robert J. Flannagan, David W. Sockice, and Lloyd Ulman, *Unionism, Economic Stabilization and Incomes Policy* (Washington: The Brookings Institution, 1983).
16. A classic work on this issue is M. Friedman and S. Kuznets, *Income from Independent Professional Practice* (New York: National Bureau for Economic Research, 1945).
17. A good review of regulations will be found in Lloyd Ulman and Robert J. Flannagan, *Wage Restraint: a Study of Incomes Policies in Western Europe* (Berkeley, California: University of California Press, 1971).
18. Daniel J. B. Mitchell provides a comprehensive presentation of both in *Unions, Wages and Inflation* (Washington: The Brookings Institution, 1980).
19. Daniel J.B. Mitchell, ibid., p. 222.
20. Clegg, ibid., pp. 345–82; and OECD, *Socially Responsible Wage Policies and Inflation: A Review of Four Countries' Experience* (Paris: OECD, 1975) pp. 49–68.
21. Barbara Wooton, *Income Policy – an Inquest and a Proposal* (London: David-Poynter, 1974) p. 60.

22. Readers who wish a more in-depth analysis of the implications of wage and price regulations should examine Daniel J. B. Mitchell's work to which reference is made above. Also, a very valuable source of high level academic economic opinion on the matter is George P. Shultz and Robert Z. Aliber (eds), *Guidelines, Informal Controls and the Market Place* (Chicago University Press, 1966).

CHAPTER 6 BARGAINING IN THE PUBLIC SECTOR

1. The classification of workers into "blue-collar" and "white-collar" categories has no economic basis. There are no job content or skill characteristics that are common to the one and not to other. The classification is social, not economic. Stanley Aronowitz has a very appropriate comment on the issue:

> 'White-collar' is a label that presupposes an essential difference between the structure of labor in the factory and in the office. It is a category of social ideology rather than of social science and has evoked the image of a system of social stratifications that regards office work as a higher status occupation than factory work, administration as more prestigious than manual labor, or, indeed, any occupation related directly to the production of goods. The bare fact is that 'white-collar' is less a description of an actual group of workers than a conceptual tool for a specific perspective on social class.

False Promises (New York: McGraw-Hill, 1973) p. 292.

2. Jack Steiber, "Collective Bargaining in the Public Sector", in Lloyd Ulman (ed.), *Challenges to Collective Bargaining* (Englewood Cliffs, N.J.: Prentice-Hall Inc., for The American Assembly, 1967) p. 87.

3. Sir Otto Kahn-Freund comments on this and related issues in *Labour Relations*, pp. 74–6.

4. Myron Lieberman, *Public-Sector Bargaining: a Policy Reappraisal* (Lexington, Mass.: Lexington Books, 1980).

5. John R. Hicks has commented that ". . . most strikes are doubtless the result of faulty negotiation", *The Theory of Wages*, (London: Macmillan, 1963) p. 146. The implication being that in most cases the range of possibilities for agreement are sufficient to facilitate agreement without a strike.

6. Harry H. Wellington and Ralph K. Winter, *The Unions and the Cities* (Washington: The Brookings Institution, 1971) pp. 8–9.

7. S. Christensen, "Pay Boards versus Collective Bargaining in the Public Sector", *Canadian Public Policy*, VI (Autumn 1980) pp. 605–13.

8. A good discussion on what can and what cannot be done in public sector bargaining, and the associated implications will be found in Harry H. Wellington and Ralph K. Winter, ibid., pp. 7–32.

9. A good source on the many issues involved is Jack Steiber, *Public Employee Unionism: Structure, Growth, Policy* (Washington, D.C.: The Brookings Institution, 1973).

10. Darold T. Barnum and I. B. Helburn, "Influencing the Electorate: Experience with Referenda on Public Employee Bargaining", *Industrial and Labor Relations Review*, XXXV (Apr. 1982) pp. 330–42.
11. In the United States very few states permit public service employees to strike. See B. V. H. Schneider, "Public Sector Labor Legislation – An Evolutionary Analysis", in Benjamin Aaron, Joseph Grodin and James L. Stern (eds), *Public Sector Bargaining* (Madison, Wisc.: Industrial Relations Research Association, 1979). Restrictions on the freedom to strike are contrary to the United Nations International Covenant on Economic, Social and Cultural Rights of 1966, and contrary to the numerous pronouncements by the International Labour Organisation Committee on Freedom of Organisation. These international organisations have taken the position that democracy cannot exist without freedom of employees to organise and without the freedom to strike.
12. Sir Otto Kahn-Freund, ibid., pp. 80–1.
13. Compare the ranking of occupations on the wage and salary scale with the social ranking in Robert W. Hodge, *et al.*, "A Comparative Study of Occupational Prestige", in R. Bendix and S. M. Lipset (eds), *Class, Status and Power* (New York: The Free Press, 1966).
14. Jean Boivin, "Collective Bargaining in the Public Sector: Some Propositions on Public Employee Unrest", in Morley Gunderson (ed.), *Collective Bargaining in Essential and Public Service Sectors*, (University of Toronto Press, 1975) pp. 4–17.
15. Jack Stieber, ibid., p. 220.
16. Jack Stieber, ibid., p. 219.
17. See statement on this issue by Benjamin Aaron in Morley Gunderson ibid., p. 105.

CHAPTER 7   ON STRIKE ACTIVITY

1. Otto Kahn-Freund, ibid., pp. 32–56.
2. For a detailed presentation on this issue see Alton W. J. Craig, *The System of Industrial Relations in Canada* (Scarborough, Ont.: Prentice-Hall Canada Inc., 1983) pp. 278–81.
3. Statistics Canada, *The Labour Force*, (Cat. No. 71-001 Monthly, Sept. 1980) p. 53.
4. Strike activity effects more workers than the numbers over whom organizations have jurisdiction, but the statistical information on "number of strikes and number of workers involved" usually refers to workers over whom the striking organization has jurisdiction.
5. See: Arthur M. Ross, "The Natural History of the Strike" in A. Kornhauser, R. Dubin and Arthur M. Ross (eds) *Industrial Conflict* (New York: McGraw-Hill, 1954) p. 23–6; Bruce E. Kaufman, "The Determinants of Strikes in the United States, 1900–1977", *Industrial & Labor Relations Review*, XXXV (July 1982) pp. 473–90; Jack W. Skeels, "The Economic and Organizational Basis of Early United States Strikes, 1900–1948", *Industrial & Labor Relations Review*, XXXV (July 1982) pp. 491–503.

6. Florence Peterson, "Review of Strikes in the United States", *Monthly Labor Review*, XLVI (May 1938) p. 1047–67; K. G. J. C. Knowles, *Strikes: a Study in Industrial Conflict* (Oxford: Blackwell, 1952); Bruce E. Kaufman, "Bargaining Theory, Inflation, and Cyclical Strike Activity in Manufacturing", *Industrial & Labor Relations Review*, XXXIV (Apr. 1981) pp. 333–5; Orley Ashenfelter and George E. Johnson, "Bargaining Theory, Trade Unions and Industrial Strike Activity", *American Economic Review*, LIX (Mar. 1969) pp. 35–49; Albert Rees, "Industrial Conflict and Business Fluctuations", *Journal of Political Economy*, LVI (Oct. 1952) pp. 371–82; Joseph Goldberg and Bernard Yabroff, "Analysis of Strikes, 1927–1949", *Monthly Labor Review*, XXX (Apr. 1977) pp. 325–41; P. K. Edwards, "Time Series Regression Models of Strike Activity: a Reconsideration with American Data", *British Journal of Industrial Relations*, XLI (Nov. 1978) pp. 320–34; Martin Paldam and Peter J. Pedersen, "The Macroeconomic Strike Model: a Study of Seventeen Countries, 1948–1975", *Industrial and Labor Relations Review*, XXXV (July 1982) pp. 504–21.

7. John Vanderkamp, "Economic Activity and Strikes in Canada", *Industrial Relations*, 9 (Feb. 1970) pp. 215–30.

8. John D. Walsh, "Economic Conditions and Strike Activity in Canada", *Industrial Relations*, 14 (Feb. 1975) pp. 45–54.

9. Ibid., p. 45.

10. Ibid., p. 46.

11. D. Sapsford, "A Time Series Analysis of U.K. Industrial Disputes", *Industrial Relations*, 14 (May 1975) pp. 242–9.

12. Sidney and Beatrice Webb suggested the legislative process and "legal enactment" as an effective way of achieving trade union objectives. See: *Industrial Democracy* (London: Longmans Green, 1902) pp. 173–221 and pp. 247–78.

13. Kaufman, ibid., p. 479.

14. Martin J. Mauro, "Strikes as a Result of Imperfect Information", *Industrial and Labor Relations Review*, XXXV (July 1982) p. 522.

15. Woodruff Imberman, "What Do Strikes Cost?", *Harvard Business Review*, LVII (May–June 1979) pp. 133–8. For estimates of output losses associated with strikes in US manufacturing industries during 1955–77 see George R. Neumann and Melvin W. Reder, "Output and Strike Activity in U.S. Manufacturing: How Large are the Losses?", *Industrial and Labor Relations Review*, XXXVII (Jan. 1984) pp. 197–211.

16. Woodruff Imberman, "Strike Costs and How to Avoid Them", *Canadian Business*, LII (Oct. 1979) pp. 130–8.

17. Parts of this section are a revised version of a paper by the author on "The Influence of Public Opinion on Labour–Management Relations and Dispute Settlement", published in *Relations Industrielles–Industrial Relations*, XXXII (1977) pp. 268–74.

18. A. W. R. Carrothers, "Industrial Relations in a New Environment", *The Conference Board Record* (Jan. 1973) p. 50.

19. Edgar L. Warren divided the public into three groups: parties, participants and outsiders. "The Role of Public Opinion in Relation to the Mediator" (Institute of Industrial Relations, University of California, Reprint no. 29, 1953) p. 1.

20. Warren, ibid.
21. Changes in public opinion and their effects during the 1920s and 1930s are discussed by H. M. Douty, "The Trend of Industrial Relations, 1922–1930", *Journal of the American Statistical Association*, XXVII (June 1932) pp. 168–72; and Milton Derber, "Growth and Expansion", in Edwin Young and Milton Derber (eds) *Labor and the New Deal* (Madison: University of Wisconsin Press, 1957) pp. 1–44.
22. The nature and effects of information in bargaining is discussed by Richard E. Walton and Robert B. McKersie, *A Behavioral Theory of Labor Negotiations* (New York: McGraw-Hill, 1965) ch. 8, pp. 281–309.
23. W. L. MacKenzie King, *Industry and Humanity* (Cambridge, Mass.: Houghton Mifflin, The University Press, 1918) p. 314 and pp. 515–16.
24. W. L. MacKenzie King, ibid., pp. 219–20.
25. Sar A. Levitan and William B. Johnston, *Work is Here to Stay, Alas* (Salt Lake City: Olympus Publishing Co., 1973).
26. R. J. Flannagan, George Straus and Lloyd Ulman, "Worker Discontent and Work Place Behaviour", *Industrial Relations*, 14 (May 1974) pp. 101–23.
27. Lloyed Zimpel (ed.), *Man Against Work*, (William B. Eardmous Publishing Co., 1974); and D. J. Cherrington, *The Work Ethic: Working Values and Values that Work* (AMACOM, 1980).
28. For a general discussion on the issue of distribution values, see Neil W. Chamberlain, *Remaking American Values* (New York: Basic Books, 1977) pp. 110–25.
29. Clark Kerr, "Educational Changes: Potential Impacts on Industrial Relations", in Industrial Relations Research Association, *The Next Twenty-Five Years of Industrial Relations* (Madison, Wisc.: 1973) pp. 187–97.
30. William F. Whyte, "Organizations for the Future", in Industrial Relations Research Association, ibid., pp. 129–46.

CHAPTER 8   TECHNOLOGY AND EMPLOYMENT ISSUES

1. Parts of this chapter are also discussed in the author's book on *Computer Technology and Employment: Retrospect and Prospect* (London: Macmillan, 1983), and in the article "The Attitude of Trade Unions Towards Technological Changes", *Relations Industrielles*, 38 (1983) pp. 104–18.
2. Trade Union Congress (TUC), *Employment and Technology* (London 1979).
3. Walter Oi examines the nature and implications of this issue in "Labor as a Quasi-Fixed Factor" in *Journal of Political Economy*, LXX (Dec. 1962) pp. 538–55.
4. Sweden has a system for the management and accommodation of change which has maintained unemployment to a minimum. The efficiency of Swedish industry suggests that the constraints on management contained in the system have not impaired management efficiency. A good description of the system will be found in Helen Ginsburg's *Full Employment and*

Public Policy: The United States and Sweden (Lexington, Mass.: Lexington Books, D.C. Heath, 1983) chs 5–7, pp. 111–60.

5. Clark Kerr, *et al.*, *Industrialism and Industrial Man* (Oxford: Oxford University Press, 1960) p. 69.

6. Philip Taft, "Internal Union Functions and Structure", in Industrial Relations Research Association, *The Next Twenty-Five Years of Industrial Relations* (Madison, Wisc., 1973) p. 1.

7. Otto Kahn-Freund made such a point (defence) in relation to the establishment of so-called restrictive labour practices. Ibid., p. 38.

8. Doris B. McLaughlin, *The Impact of Labor Unions on the Rate and Direction of Technological Innovations* (Institute of Labor and Industrial Relations, The University of Michigan-Wayne State University, Ann Arbor, Michigan, Feb. 1979).

9. Originally identified by Sumner H. Slichter, James J. Healy and E. Robert Livernash in *Impact of Collective Bargaining on Management* (Washington, D.C.: The Brookings Institution, 1960).

10. Doris B. McLaughlin, Ibid., Table 1, p. 29.

11. Ibid., p. 99.

12. A report on technological changes in four British companies indicates that in none of them was the technical change negotiated. The changes caused redundancies, effected working practices, caused changes in job descriptions, and changes in both manning levels and grading, yet no negotiations preceded the introduction of the technological changes. Whatever bargaining takes place, is usually *after* the technical changes have been introduced. Roy Moore and Hugo Levie, "The Impact of New Technology on Trade Union Organization", in Commission of the European Community, *Social Change and Technology in Europe: Information Bulletin No. 8* (Brussels: October 1982) pp. 32–54.

13. An excellent source on this issue is Simon Rottenberg (ed.), *Occupational Licensure and Regulation* (Washington: American Enterprise Institute for Public Policy Research, 1980).

14. Stephen G. Peitchinis, *Labour–Management Relations in the Railway Industry* (Task Force on Labour Relations, Study No. 20, Information Canada, Ottawa, 1971) p. 297.

15. A good examination of the assumptions underlying discussions of featherbedding is provided by Ivar Berg and James Kuhn in "The Assumptions of Featherbedding", *Labor Law Journal* (Apr. 1962) pp. 227–83.

16. Milton Friedman, *Capitalism and Freedom* (Chicago University Press, 1962) pp. 137–60.

17. R. B. McKersie and L. C. Hunter, *Pay, Productivity and Collective Bargaining* (New York: Macmillan, 1973).

Selected Bibliography

Aaron, B., Grodin, J. R. and Stern, J. L. (eds), *Public Sector Bargaining*, Industrial Relations Research Association Series (Washington, DC: Bureau of National Affairs, 1979).

Bacharach, S. and Lawler, E. J., *Bargaining: Power, Tactics and Outcomes* (San Francisco: Jossey-Bass Publishers, 1981).

Bakke, E. W., Kerr, C. and Anrod, C. W., *Unions, Management and the Public* (New York: Harcourt, Brace & World, 1967).

Barbush, J., *American Unions: Structure, Government and Politics* (New York: Random House, 1976).

Benson, I. and Lloyd, J., *New Technology and Industrial Change: the Impact of the Scientific-Technical Revolution on Labour and Industry* (New York: Nichols, 1983).

Brown, E. H. Phelps, *The Growth of British Industrial Relations* (London: Macmillan, 1959).

Bulletin of Comparative Labour Relations, Special Issue, vol. 12, 1983, *Technological Change and Industrial Relations*.

Burns, T. R., Karlsson, L. E. and Rus, V. (eds), *Work and Power: the Liberation of Work and the Control of Political Power* (Beverly Hills, Cal.: Sage Publications, 1979).

Carby-Hall, J. R., *Worker Participation in Europe* (London: Croom Helm, 1977).

Chamberlain, N. and Kuhn, J., *Collective Bargaining* (New York: McGraw-Hill, 1965).

Chitayat, G., *Trade Union Mergers and Labor Conglomerates* (New York: Praeger Publishers, 1979).

Clegg, H. A., *The Changing System of Industrial Relations in Great Britain* (Oxford: Basil Blackwell, 1979).

Commission on Industrial Relations, *Workers' Participation and Collective Bargaining in Europe* (London: HMSO, 1974).

Crouch, L. and Pizzorno, A. (eds), *The Resurgence of Class Conflict in Western Europe since 1968* (London: Macmillan, 1978).

Dunlop, J. T., *Industrial Relations Systems* (New York: Henry Hold, 1958).

Dunlop, J. T. and Galenson, W. (eds), *Labor in the Twentieth Century* (New York: The Academic Press, 1978).

Edwards, P. K., *Strikes in the United States, 1881–1974* (New York: St. Martin's Press, 1981).

Edwards, P. K. and Scullion, H., *The Social Organization of Industrial Conflict* (Oxford: Basil Blackwell, 1982).

Ewing, D. W., *"Do It My Way or You're Fired!": Employee Rights and the Changing Role of Management Prerogatives* (New York: John Wiley, 1983).

Fogel, W. (ed.), *Job Equity and Other Studies in Industrial Relations: Essays in Honor of Frederic Meyers* (Los Angeles, Cal.: Institute of Industrial Relations, University of California, 1982).

Forseback, L., *Industrial Relations and Employment in Sweden* (Stockholm: The Swedish Institute, 1976).

Freedman, A., *Managing Labor Relations* (New York: The Conference Board, 1979).

Ginsburg, H., *Full Employment and Public Policy in the United States and Sweden* (Lexington, Mass.: D. C. Heath, 1983).

Gunderson, Morley (ed.), *Collective Bargaining in Essential and Public Service Sectors* (University of Toronto Press, 1975).

Healy, J. (ed.), *Creative Collective Bargaining: Meeting Today's Challenges to Labor-Management Relations* (Englewood Cliffs, NJ: Prentice-Hall, 1965).

Herman, E. E. and Kuhn, A., *Collective Bargaining and Labor Relations* (Englewood Cliffs, NJ: Prentice-Hall, 1981).

Hill, S., *Competition and Control at Work: the New Industrial Sociology* (The MIT Press, 1981).

Jamieson, S. M., *Industrial Conflict in Canada* (Ottawa: Economic Council of Canada, 1979).

Kahn-Freund, Otto, *Labour Relations: Heritage and Adjustment* (Oxford University Press, 1979).

Kassalow, E. M., *Trade Unions and Industrial Relations: an International Comparison* (New York: Random House, 1969).

Kerr, C. et. al., *Industrialism and Industrial Man* (Cambridge, Mass.: Harvard University Press, 1966).

King, C. D. and Van de Vall, M., *Models of Industrial Democracy: Consultation, Co-determination and Workers' Management* (The Hague: Mouton Publishers, 1978).

Kochan, T. A., Mitchell, D. J. B. and Dyer, L. (eds), *Industrial Relations Research in the 1970's: Review and Appraisal* (Madison, Wisc.: Industrial Relations Research Association, 1982).

Kornhauser, A. et al. (eds), *Industrial Conflict* (New York: McGraw-Hill, 1954).

Kuhne, Robert J., *Co-Determination in Business: Workers' Representatives in Business* (New York: Praeger, 1980).

Lewis, H. Gregg, *Unionism and Relative Wages in the United States* (University of Chicago Press, 1963).

Lieberman, Myron, *Public-Sector Bargaining: a Policy Reappraisal* (Lexington Books, 1980).

Mills, Daniel Quinn, *Labor–Management Relations* (New York: McGraw-Hill, 1978).

Mitchell, Daniel, J. B., *Unions, Wages and Inflation* (Washington, DC: The Brookings Institution, 1980).

OECD, *Collective Bargaining and Government Policies* (Paris: 1979).

Peitchinis, Stephen G., *Labour-Management Relations in the Railway Industry* (Ottawa: Information Canada, 1971).

Peitchinis, Stephen G., *Computer Technology and Employment: Retrospect and Prospect* (London: Macmillan, 1983).

Ross, A. M. and Hartman, P. T., *Changing Patterns of Industrial Conflict*, (New York: John Wiley, 1960).

Rottenberg, Simon (ed.), *Occupational Licensure and Regulation* (Washington, DC:

American Enterprise Institute for Public Policy Research, 1980).

Slichter, S. J., Healy, J. and Livernash, E., *The Impact of Collective Bargaining on Management* (Washington, DC: The Brookings Institution, 1960).

Sommers, G. G. (ed.), *The Next Twenty-Five Years of Industrial Relations* (Madison, Wisc.: Industrial Relations Research Association, 1973).

Stieber, Jack, *Public Employee Unionism: Structure, Growth, Policy* (Washington, DC: The Brookings Institution, 1973).

Stieber, J. and McKersie, R. B. (eds), *U.S. Industrial Relations 1950–1980: A Critical Assessment* (Madison, Wisc.: Industrial Relations Research Association, 1981).

Storey, J., *Managerial Prerogative and the Question of Control*, (Boston, Mass.: Routledge & Kegan Paul, 1983).

Taylor, R., *Workers and The New Depression* (London: Macmillan, 1982).

Thurow, Lester C., *Generating Inequality: Mechanisms of Distribution in the U.S. Economy* (New York: Basic Books, 1975).

Turner, H. A., Roberts, G. and Roberts, D., *Management Characteristics and Labour Conflict* (Cambridge University Press, 1977).

Ulman, Lloyd and Robert J. Flanagan, *Wage Restraint: a Study of Incomes Policies in Western Europe* (Los Angeles: University of California Press, 1971).

Usher, Dan, *The Economic Prerequisite for Democracy* (London: Basil Blackwell, 1981).

Weber, A. (ed.), *The Structure of Collective Bargaining* (Glencoe, Ill.: The Free Press, 1960).

Index